The 2nd Res

THE 2nd
Restaurant
RECIPE
BOOK

Absolute Press

Published by Absolute Press (publishers)
14 Widcombe Crescent, Widcombe Hill, Bath,
Avon. BA2 6AH.

Editors **Jon Croft**
       Sarah Croft

© Absolute Press (publishers)

First published 1982

Illustrations: Carl Willson, MSIAD

Art assistant: Marianne Williams

Printed by Graphic Print, Springwater House,
Moy Road, Taffs Well, Cardiff.

The publishers would like to thank KITCHENS of
Bath who kindly loaned the kitchen equipment
which appears on the cover of this book.

ISBN 0 9506785 4 6

Contents

Introduction

When the original 'Restaurant Recipe Book' was first published in November 1982 neither the contributors nor the editors had any idea of the kind of response that was to follow. Its success was immediate and widespread. Enthusiastic cooks from all over the country bought and used and enjoyed it. Copies have been sent to all parts of the world. Now, because of persistent requests, a follow up book has been compiled, 'The 2nd Restaurant Recipe Book'.

If anything, this second recipe book is even better than the first. Many of the restaurants are the same, some are different. All have spent considerable time in planning the three recipes that they have each contributed.

The format, as before, is straightforward and simple. Each restaurant chef has planned and provided a three course dinner party menu which appears on a double-page spread. The varying styles and influences of each contributor means that each double-page has its own character.

The editors would like to thank all the chefs for their enthusiasm and skills which have made 'The 2nd Restaurant Recipe Book' possible. 'The 2nd Restaurant Recipe Book' is a tribute to the outstanding talents that are to be found amongst West Country chefs.

Bon appétit.

Ainslie's

Bath
Chef *David Mott*

Spicy Tomato Soup   *Serves 4*

4 oz. (125g.) butter
1 large onion, chopped
½ teaspoon ground black pepper
1 teaspoon paprika
1½ teaspoon ground mace
4 or 5 cloves, crushed
1 oz. (25g.) flour
2 or 3 bay leaves
1 teaspoon mixed herbs
½ teaspoon sugar
1 tablespoon tomato purée
1½ lb. (875g.) ripe tomatoes, chopped
2 pints (generous litre) chicken stock
1 glass port
tabasco (optional), double cream and
    chopped parsley to garnish
salt

This may sound hot, but it really is deliciously spicy — very good for cold winter evenings.

1 Sweat the chopped onion in butter. Add the black pepper, paprika, mace, flour and cloves and singe, taking care not to scorch.

2 Add the chicken stock and tomatoes and bring to the boil. Add the bay leaves, mixed herbs, sugar, purée, tabasco and salt and return to the boil and allow to boil slowly for 15 minutes.

3 After 15 minutes, add the port, remove the bay leaves and liquidise. Pass through a strainer and pour into bowls. Serve with chopped parsley and a ribbon of cream.

Pork with Prunes

1½ - 2 lb. (675g. - 900g.) pork
   tenderloin, trimmed
2 oz. (50g.) butter
½ pint (275ml.) water
1 pint (575ml.) red wine
32 small dried prunes
2 tablespoons redcurrant jelly
1 teaspoon paprika
½ teaspoon mixed herbs
¼ pint (150ml.) double cream
salt and pepper
parsley, chopped

Don't be put off by the sound of the prunes; with the wine and cream reduction they produce a wonderful rich, plummy sauce. Very popular at our restaurant.

1 Pour the red wine and water into a deep saucepan and bring to the boil. Add the redcurrant jelly and prunes and simmer for at least 30 minutes, the wine and water should reduce to no less than ½ pint (275ml.) liquor. (For best results, leave the prunes to soak overnight, they will then absorb a lot of the liquor and become plump).

2 Slice the pork into ½" (1 cm.) medallions. Melt the butter in a frying pan, add the pork and sprinkle with paprika, mixed herbs and lightly fry for 2 minutes or until the pork is almost cooked.

3 Remove the pork from the pan and add the prunes and the liquor, turn up the heat and allow to reduce. When there is about 3 - 4 tablespoons of liquor, return the pork to the pan and add the cream. Bring to the boil and allow to reduce slightly and correct the seasoning. There should only be a small amount of sauce for each portion. Serve with chopped parsley.

Strawberry Meringue

3 egg whites
½ lb. (225g.) caster sugar
½ pint (275ml.) whipping cream
½ lb. (225g.) ripe strawberries
½ lb. (225g.) vanilla ice cream

1 Whisk the egg whites and 6 oz. (175g.) of the sugar until very stiff. Pipe out 4 meringue nests and dry in a warm place for 6 - 7 hours or until crisp.

2 Liquidise the strawberries, saving 4 for decoration.

3 Whip the cream with the remaining sugar until the cream is fluffy. Carefully fold in the strawberry purée and place in a fridge for 30 minutes.

4 To make, scoop 2 oz. (50g.) of ice cream into each meringue nest and spoon a quarter of the strawberry fool mixture over each portion. Then cut each of the 4 strawberries that you saved and decorate. Need we say more?

Anthony's

Bristol
Chef/proprietor *Anthony Van der Woerd*

Mushroom and Watercress Pâté

Serves 4

1½ large onions, finely chopped
1 oz. (25g.) butter to cook
4 oz. (125g.) mushrooms, finely
   chopped
salt and pepper
dash Tabasco
6 oz. (175g.) watercress, finely chopped
2 cloves garlic, crushed
6 oz. (175g.) curd cheese
1 oz. (25g.) soft butter
lemon and watercress to garnish

1 Sauté the onions and garlic in the butter
until soft. Add the mushrooms briefly at high
heat. Add the watercress and cook until it
begins to go limp, about one minute. Cool.

2 Blend well together by hand and put into
ramekins. Garnish with the lemon and
watercress.

Chicken Breasts in Whisky Sauce

Serves 6

6 chicken breasts
salt and pepper
lemon juice
2 oz. (50g.) melted butter

For the sauce:
2 tablespoons chicken stock
¼ pint (150ml.) double cream
whisky
julienne of carrots, celery, leeks,
   blanched

1 Place the chicken breasts in a well buttered ovenproof pan. Sprinkle sparingly with salt and pepper and squeeze over the lemon juice. Dot with butter.

2 Place in a hot oven, closely covered with foil, for 15 - 20 minutes until the flesh is set firm. Strain off two-thirds of the liquid and place on heat. Flame with whisky, add the stock, julienne of vegetables and cream and reduce sauce rapidly until thickened. Add more whisky and salt and pepper if desired and serve.

Chocolate Roulade with Brandy

7 oz. (200g.) semi-sweet plain
   chocolate
1 teaspoon instant coffee
5 eggs (size 3), separated
5 oz. (150g.) caster sugar
oil for brushing
3 tablespoons water
½ pint (275ml.) double cream
pinch sugar
brandy
icing sugar

1 Beat the egg yolks and sugar in an electric mixer until light and fluffy, at high speed — approximately 5 minutes.

2 Melt the chocolate and coffee in water and add to the beaten egg. Whip the egg whites until stiff and fold quickly into the chocolate and egg mix.

3 Pour this mixture into an 8 x 10'' (20 x 25cm.) Swiss roll tin which has been lined with oiled greaseproof paper. Bake in a moderate oven for 20 - 30 minutes. Allow to cool and shrink.

4 Brush the crust with a little water to soften. Whip the cream, sugar and brandy until stiff and spread over the sponge. Take hold of the backing paper and start to roll up the sponge, peeling off as you go. Sprinkle with icing sugar and serve.

Beaujolais

Bath
Chef/proprietor *Philippe Wall*

Chicken Satay

Serves 8

2 lb. (900g.) chicken breasts
½ cup coconut milk

For the marinade:
3 slices ginger, crushed
3 cloves garlic, crushed
1 tablespoon curry powder
1 tablespoon coriander powder
1 teaspoon salt
2 tablespoons butter
3 tablespoons light cream

For the sauce:
1 tablespoon red curry paste
1 tablespoon chilli sauce
1 tablespoon sugar
2 tablespoons peanut butter
1½ cups coconut milk or cream
1 tablespoon lemon juice
1 teaspoon salt

1 Cut the chicken breasts into 1″ (2.5cm.) strips and knead with the marinade ingredients, one at a time. Leave to marinate for at least 2 hours.

2 Thread a few pieces of chicken on to the top half of a satay stick. Cook the threaded chicken over charcoal or under a grill. Whilst cooking, sprinkle with coconut milk. Serve with the sauce.

3 Make the sauce by heating the coconut milk until boiling. Add the curry and chilli paste and stir fry. Add peanut butter, sugar, salt and lemon juice. The sauce should have a salty, sweet and a little sour taste. Chicken satay makes an excellent hors d'oeuvre served with a cucumber salad.

Poulet à l'Estragon

4 - 5 lb. (1¾ - 2¼ kilos) chicken
2 large sprigs tarragon or tablespoon
   dry
1/3 bottle dry white wine
salt to taste
2 good sprinkles black pepper
oil and butter
1 cup double cream

1 Remove the breasts and wings, joint legs
and cut all in half to make extra portions.

2 In an ovenproof cast iron casserole, heat
a little oil with a knob of butter. Fry the
chicken pieces. When nice and golden, add
salt, pepper and tarragon and put into the
oven for 10 minutes at 200°C/400°F/gas 6.

3 Take out and add the wine. Pop back into
the oven for another 15 minutes or until
ready, with the lid on.

4 Remove from oven, take off lid and put on
a moderate heat. Add cream and stir until
nice and unctuous. Serve with rice or
sautéed potatoes.

Reine-Claudes au Syrop

20 greengages
5 oz. (150g.) sugar
pint (575ml.) water
1 large wine glass brandy
½ teaspoon green peppercorns

1 Simmer the fruit in the water, with the
sugar, for a maximum of 15 minutes.

2 Take the fruit out and place in a bowl. Add
the green peppercorns to the syrup and
reduce to a little under two-thirds of the
original amount. Mix in the brandy.

3 Pour the strained syrup over the fruit and
cool. Chill in a refrigerator. Serve with rich
double cream or a crème Chantilly.

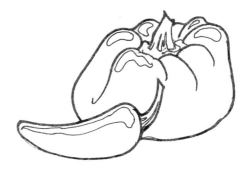

Beechfield House

Beanacre
Chef/proprietor *Peter Crawford-Rolt*

Garden Pumpkin Soup

Serves 12

1 x 8 - 10 lb. (5 - 6 kilo) pumpkin
2 lb. (900g.) yellow split peas
4 oz. (125g.) fat bacon, chopped
1 lb. (450g.) onions, cut into small cubes
1 lb. (450g.) carrots, cut into small cubes
1 lb. (450g.) leeks, cut into small cubes
½ lb. (225g.) celery, cut into small
   cubes

4 cloves garlic, chopped
4 bay leaves
2 oz. (50g.) butter
4 pints (2¼ litres) chicken stock or
   bouillon cubes
½ pint (275ml.) double cream
pastry to seal the pumpkin lid
salt, pepper and grated nutmeg

1 Cut a lid from the pumpkin at a 45 degree angle. Remove seeds. Scoop out flesh, leaving approximately half the depth — care should be taken not to puncture the shell. Keep the shell and lid.

2 Sweat the vegetables in butter along with the bacon, pumpkin flesh, garlic and bay leaves. Add the split peas, chicken stock and bring to the boil and simmer for about 1½ hours or until the split peas are tender. Remove bay leaves.

3 Liquidise the mixture and season with milled pepper, a little grated nutmeg and salt. Simmer and add the cream, and whilst still simmering add to the pumpkin. Seal with the pastry and place in a medium oven for 15 - 20 minutes, removing before the shell goes soft. Serve with croûtons.

Marinated Breast of Chicken with a Saffron and Sorrel Cream Sauce

Serves 6

6 chicken supremes
½ pint (275ml.) double cream
pinch saffron
2 oz. (50g.) sorrel leaves, finely
   shredded
2 fl.oz. (50ml.) chicken glaze, prepared
   from the carcass (or ½ teaspoon
   chicken bouillon)
2 fl.oz. (50ml.) white wine

For the marinade:
1 cup dry white wine
½ cup olive oil
1 clove garlic, chopped
½ teaspoon salt
juice and grated rind 1 lime
1 teaspoon fresh tarragon, rosemary or
   basil, chopped finely
3 pieces star anise (available from
   health food shops)

1 Marinate the prepared chicken breasts for 1 day.

2 Place each breast on a square of foil, shiny surface inwards and wrap into envelopes. Place the envelopes onto a baking tray and bake in a medium oven for approximately 10 minutes, according to size. A slight pinkness is perfection.

3 Meanwhile place the cream, white wine, saucepan and reduce by half. Draw to one side.

4 Slice the cooked chicken breasts into 10 thin slices each and fan out on plates. Reheat the sauce, add the finely shredded sorrel and cook for 30 seconds and check seasoning. Serve the sauce either separately or coat the chicken breasts.

Pitch Lake Pudding

Serves 6

5 eggs, separated
½ lb. (225g.) caster sugar
4 oz. (125g.) unsweetened cocoa
2 tablespoons instant coffee
6 tablespoons dark rum
½ pint (275ml.) double cream
pinch salt

This was an inspiration which came from a visit to Trinidad's natural ash-felt lake.

1 Place the cocoa in a large basin over hot water.

2 Dissolve the coffee in ¼ pint (150ml.) boiling water, add the sugar and stir until dissolved. Add to the cocoa and stir for 5 minutes.

3 Whisk in the egg yolks one at a time until volume increases, then remove from the heat and add the rum.

4 Add the salt to the egg whites and whisk until they peak. Fold into cocoa mixture gently. Pour into individual glasses or a large bowl. Refrigerate overnight.

5 Before serving, lightly whip cream until it just flows and pour on top of glasses. Serve with almond biscuits (ratafias).

Bistro Twenty One

Bristol
Chef/proprietor *Stephen Markwick*

Spinach and Cream Cheese Pancakes

1½ - 2 lb. (675 - 900g.) leaf spinach
½ lb. (225g.) cream cheese
2 oz. (50g.) Emmantal, grated
salt, pepper and nutmeg
little double cream

For the batter:
¼ lb. (125g.) flour
1 egg
½ pint (275ml.) milk
1 oz. (25g.) butter
salt and pepper

1 Wash the spinach well and strip off the stalks. Place in a pan and cook until tender. Put through a mincer.

2 Mix the spinach with the cream cheese, most of the Emmantal and the seasoning.

3 Make the pancakes.

4 Spread the spinach mixture over the pancakes and roll, allowing 2 pancakes per person. Place in one large dish or individual dishes, cover with a little cream and the remaining cheese and bake in a medium oven until bubbling.

Venison and Steak Pie

Serves 6 - 8

3 lb. (1¼ kilos) shoulder venison
1 lb. (450g.) good stewing steak
½ lb. (225g.) streaky bacon, cut into
    lardons
¼ lb. (125g.) button onions
¼ lb. (125g.) mushrooms
good stock
tomato purée
1 lb. (450g.) shortcrust pastry

For the marinade:
½ pint (275ml.) red wine
2 fl.oz. (50ml.) olive oil
2 fl.oz. (50ml.) red wine vinegar
1 onion, chopped
4 garlics, chopped
thyme
6 - 9 juniper berries, crushed

This pie can be made even better with the addition of further game, such as hare or pheasant. The marinade ingredients are really a guide and can easily be added to with anything that you fancy.

1 Cut and trim the venison and beef into good size pieces and marinade for at least 1 day — it will keep in the marinade for much longer.

2 Drain meat and seal well in very hot frying pan. Put into casserole. Fry the vegetables from the marinade and add. Add a little flour and some tomato purée, also the juices from the marinade, stock and possibly some more red wine. Bring to the boil , check seasoning and simmer, covered, in a cool oven for 1 - 1½ hours.

3 Toss the streaky bacon, button onions and mushrooms in frying pan and add to the casserole about 20 - 25 minutes before the end of cooking.

4 When the casserole is done, leave to cool and put into a pie dish. Cover with the pastry and bake in a hot oven for about 30 minutes.

Poached Figs with Pernod

2 - 3 figs per person
Pernod

For the syrup:
1 pint (575ml.) water
1 lb. (450g.) granulated sugar
zest of 1 lemon

1 Make a syrup by bringing the above ingredients to the boil and simmer gently for about 10 minutes.

2 Add the figs and poach lightly until just cooked. Remove and place in a large bowl to avoid squashing the fruit. Sprinkle with Pernod whilst still hot.

3 Reduce the syrup further and then strain over the figs. Serve cold with lightly whipped cream.

Blostin's

Shepton Mallet
Chef/proprietor *Bill Austin*

Baked Eggs with Salami

Serves 1

2 eggs
1 slice salami, skinned and diced
1 teaspoonful fresh double cream
salt and black pepper
parsley, freshly chopped

1 Put the diced salami into a ramekin.
Sprinkle with chopped parsley and season
with black pepper and salt if required — you
should check the saltiness of the salami in
order to judge how much salt you will need to
use. Crack 2 eggs on top and dribble the
cream over.

2 Bake in a hot oven until done to
preference — runny is best. Serve garnished
with more parsley.

Wild Rabbit in White Wine and French Mustard

Serves 4

2 small wild rabbits, jointed
1 large onion, roughly chopped
1 garlic, crushed
1 stick celery, roughly chopped
bouquet garni
leek, finely chopped
seasoned flour
1 tablespoon French mustard
1 bottle dry white wine
1 dessertspoon double cream
salt and black pepper
pinch thyme

18

oil to cook
croûtons to garnish
freshly chopped parsley to garnish

In the restaurant we often use a dry English vineyard wine. In two years time our own recently planted vineyard should be producing wine for this excellent dish — weather permitting!

1 Heat the oil in a frying pan and throw in the garlic and vegetables and lightly sauté for a few minutes. Remove to a Le Creûset or similar casserole dish with a lid.

2 Roll the joints of rabbit in the seasoned flour. Fry in the hot oil in the frying pan. Add to the casserole on the bed of vegetables.

3 Deglaze the frying pan with a cupful of wine. Add to the casserole.

4. In a bowl, dilute the mustard with the remaining wine and add to the casserole. Add the bouquet garni, seasoning and thyme. Cover the casserole and put in a moderate oven and leave for about 30 minutes or until cooked.

5 Transfer the rabbit joints to a serving dish. Over a high heat reduce the sauce with the vegetables by half. Take off the heat and stir in the double cream. Pour over the rabbit joints and garnish with croûtons and freshly chopped parsley.

Passion Fruit and Lime Sorbet

Serves 4

4 oz. (125g.) caster sugar
½ pint (275ml.) water
2 limes
3 cooking apples, peeled and cored
2 egg whites
½ pint (275ml.) passion fruit pulp (about 16), reserving a little for decoration

1 Boil the sugar, water and rinds of limes for 10 minutes. Strain and cool.

2 Cook the apples in lime juice. Liquidise and cool. Add the apple and lime purée to the syrup. Add the passion fruit pulp and place in the freezer. When it begins to set, whisk the egg whites and fold in. Freeze until set.

3 15 minutes before serving, transfer to a refrigerator to soften slightly.

4 Decorate with strained passion fruit juice poured over.

Bowlish House

Shepton Mallet
Chef *Janine McKay*

Paprika Aubergines

Serves 4

2 medium sized aubergines, roughly
  chopped
1 large onion, finely chopped
1 14 - 15 oz. (400 - 425g.) tin tomatoes
2 cloves garlic, crushed
1 oz. (25g.) butter
1 oz. (25g.) brown breadcrumbs
salt and pepper to taste
1 tablespoon paprika
oil for frying

1 Sauté the onion and garlic until the onion is transparent. Add the tomatoes and simmer until the sauce is reduced and fairly thick. Remove any tomato skins or stalks.

2 Meanwhile, slice the aubergines into sensible sized pieces and deep fry until browned. Drain well on absorbent paper and add to the reduced tomato and onion mixture. Season with salt and pepper and add paprika.

3 Simmer for 5 minutes and place aubergine mix in individual serving dishes. Sprinkle with breadcrumbs and top with butter and perhaps a pinch of extra paprika. Lightly grill until the breadcrumbs are crisp and toasted.

Calves' Liver with Gin and Lime Sauce

Serves 4

1 lb. (450g.) calves' liver, very thinly
  sliced
seasoned flour
oil and 1 oz. (25g.) butter for frying

For the gin and lime sauce:
¾ pint (425ml.) beef stock
½ oz. (15g.) butter
¼ lb. (125g.) onion, finely chopped
grated rind and juice 3 limes, or lemon if
  unavailable
2 tablespoons gin
dash Worcester sauce
1 rounded tablespoon arrowroot (mixed
  with some of the stock)

For the Karen carrots:
1 lb. (450g.) carrots, washed and
  trimmed
1 oz. (25g.) butter
1 tablespoon salt
1 tablespoon lemon juice
1 tablespoon clear honey
parsley, finely chopped

1 Make the sauce by melting the butter in a heavy bottomed pan and lightly sauté the onion till soft. Gradually blend in the other ingredients and simmer for 30 minutes. Liquidise until smooth and keep warm.

2 Coat the liver slices with the flour and lightly fry in the oil and butter mix. A light cooking is all that is necessary and the liver is done when small bubbles of blood burst through. Cook each side equally. Serve with some of the sauce poured over and the remainder in a sauce boat. Accompany with the Karen carrots.

3 If using small, new carrots, leave whole, otherwise cut into fingers. Bring to the boil with only enough salted water to barely cover. Simmer for 5 - 10 minutes until just tender. In another saucepan gently melt the butter and add the lemon juice, honey and parsley, blending well together. Drain the carrots and toss lightly in the honey and lemon butter until evenly coated. Serve immediately.

Crème Velour

Serves 6

2½ oz. (60g.) good dark chocolate
6 oz. (175g.) cream cheese
1½ oz. (40g.) caster sugar
½ pint (275ml.) double cream
1 tablespoon brandy

1 Soften the cream cheese. Add the sugar and whisk until smooth.

2 Melt the chocolate with a few drops of water in a bowl over a simmering pan half full of water. Add the melted chocolate to the cream cheese and whisk so that the mixture remains smooth.

3 Lightly whip the cream and fold into the cheese and chocolate mixture. Flavour with the brandy and give a final whisk until the mixture forms soft peaks. Put into serving dishes or glasses and serve chilled.

Castle Hotel

Taunton
Chef *John Hornsby*

Chilled Beetroot Soup with Tomato and Basil Sorbet

Serves 4 - 6

2 pints (generous litre) chicken stock
3 lb. (1.5 kilo) fresh washed beetroot,
   roughly sliced
bayleaf
2 egg whites
6 leaves gelatine
6 peppercorns
pinch salt to season
chervil to garnish

For the sorbet:
¼ pint (150ml.) tomato juice
dash Worcester sauce
fresh basil, shredded
equal quantities crushed ice and salt

The three dishes that appear on these two pages were specially cooked by me for the luncheon at the Inn on the Park in November 1982 to launch the Silver Jubilee edition of the Egon Ronay Guide.

1 In a large saucepan put the chicken stock, roughly sliced beetroot, bayleaf, egg whites, leaf gelatine and peppercorns. Whisk to the boil and then reduce the heat. The egg whites will rise to the surface and clear the stock. Simmer for 1 - 1½ hours.

2 Strain through a tammy cloth or a glass cloth. Place into a bowl and leave to cool. When cool, place into the refrigerator. The stock will set lightly. Correct seasoning.

3 Make the water ice by filling a bowl with equal quantities of crushed ice and salt. Pour the Worcester sauce and tomato juice into a stainless steel or china bowl. Place on the crushed ice and salt. Whisk slowly until set. Finish by adding shredded fresh basil.

4 To serve, place the soup into serving bowls and arrange 4 chervil leaves around the rim of the bowls. Place a spoon of the water ice on top and serve.

Sliced Fillet of Lamb with Somerset Herbs

Serves 4

1¼ lb. (575g.) loin of lamb, well trimmed
¼ lb. (125g.) butter
¾ pint (425ml.) reduced brown veal
    stock
¾ pint (425ml.) white wine
chopped herbs — tarragon, rosemary,
    thyme, basil, mint and parsley
seasoning

1 Reduce the white wine and add the
chopped herbs. Pour in the reduced veal
stock. Thicken the sauce by adding the hard
butter slowly, whisking continuously.

2 Season the lamb and fry quickly in butter
for 3 - 4 minutes, moving all the time. Be sure
to keep the lamb pink.

3 To serve, slice the lamb and arrange on
dinner plates. Pour the sauce over.

John Hornsby's Bread and Butter Pudding

Serves 4 - 6

¾ pint (425ml.) milk
¼ pint (150ml.) single cream
2 whole eggs
2 oz. (50g.) sugar
6 slices buttered French bread, ¼"
    (1cm.) thick
1 oz. (25g.) currants
1 oz. (25g.) sultanas
dash vanilla essence
nutmeg
apricot jam

1 Mix the cream, sugar, vanilla essence,
eggs and a pinch of nutmeg in a glass or
china bowl.

2 Boil the milk and pour onto the mixture.

3 Line the bottom of an oven-proof dish with
the bread. Add the sultanas and currants
and pour the egg mixture over the bread.

4 Place the dish in a roasting tray of water
and cook for 35 - 45 minutes in a moderate
oven. Remove when set, the bread should
have risen to the top. Brush the top with
boiling jam and serve.

Cleeveway House

Bishops Cleeve
Chef/proprietor *John Marfell*

Iced Cucumber Soup

Serves 4

1 large cucumber
½ pint (225g.) yoghurt
3 cloves garlic
2 tablespoons tarragon vinegar
½ pint (275ml.) double cream
salt and pepper
10 oz. (275g.) ice cubes

1 In a food processor or liquidiser, blend together the cucumber, garlic, yoghurt and vinegar. Stir in the cream and season to taste.

2 Add the ice cubes to the soup and chill. The ice should melt a little and the soup will be deliciously cold on serving.

Pork Normande

2 pork tenderloins
24 cup mushrooms
4 oz. (125g.) butter
3 fl. oz. (75ml.) Calvados
cup thick double cream
salt and pepper

1 Cut up the tenderloin into ½″ (1 cm.) rounds. Season on both sides with salt and pepper.

2 Melt the butter and lightly brown the pork and mushrooms. Add the Calvados, cover and cook in a hot oven, 220°C/425°F/gas 7 for 5 minutes.

3 When cooked, remove from the oven and add the cream to the juices and combine and reduce to desired consistency. Check seasoning and serve.

Blackcurrant Ice Cream

4 eggs, separated
½ lb. (225g.) caster sugar
1 pint (575ml.) double cream
12 oz. (350g.) blackcurrants

1 Stew and sieve the blackcurrants to make a purée. Allow to cool.

2 Whip up the cream to soft peaks and whip in the egg yolks. Combine with the purée.

3 Whip up the egg whites with the sugar and fold this meringue mixture into the fruit and cream. Freeze and serve.

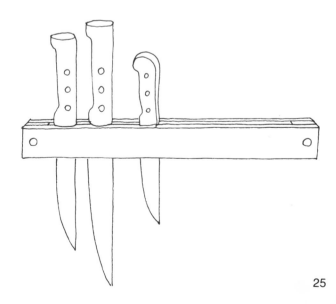

Country Elephant

Painswick
Chef/proprietor *Jane Medforth*

Aubergine Fritters with Tomato Mayonnaise   *Serves 4*

1 - 2 aubergine, sliced into ¼'' (1 cm.)
   slices, allowing 5 - 6 slices per portion

For the batter:
2 oz. (50g.) plain flour
1½ tablespoons oil
water to mix
1 egg white, stiffly beaten

For the tomato mayonnaise:
½ pint (275ml.) home-made
   mayonnaise
tomato purée, to taste
lemon juice, to taste
tabasco, to taste

1 Sprinkle lightly with salt and leave for 30 minutes to degorge.

2 Prepare the batter by sifting the flour. Make a well and add the oil. Beat, adding the water when necessary, until the consistency of lightly whipped cream. Just before using, add the stiffly beaten egg white.

3 Remove the moisture from the aubergine with kitchen paper. Dip the slices in seasoned flour and then into the batter. Fry, preferably in a deep fat fryer, at 180°C/ 350°F, turning once, until crisp and golden.

4 Drain the aubergine on kitchen paper and serve at once on a lettuce leaf with a lemon wedge. Serve the tomato mayonnaise separately.

Sautéed Monkfish in White Wine and Cream Sauce

Serves 4

4 small fillets monkfish, cut into diagonal
    slices ¼'' (1cm.) thick
approximately 2 oz. (50g.) butter
approximately 4 tablespoons white wine
approximately 4 tablespoons double
    cream
seasoned flour
salt and pepper
chopped parsley
lemon wedges

1 Dip the fish slices in the seasoned flour, removing any excess.

2 Melt the butter in a sauté pan and add the fish. Fry until a light golden brown, turning once. Season with salt and pepper and add the wine, enough to cover the bottom of the pan. Poach until tender, about 5 minutes. Add the cream and boil up well to thicken the sauce.

3 Transfer fish to a serving dish and pour over the sauce. Sprinkle with parsley and serve at once accompanied with lemon wedges.

Coffee and Hazelnut Ice Cream

Serves 4

3 eggs, separated
¼ pint (150ml.) double cream
3 oz. (75g.) caster sugar
3 oz. (75g.) hazelnuts, shelled, toasted
    and chopped
1 dessertspoon Camp coffee essence

1 Whisk the egg yolks and cream together until thick. Add the coffee essence.

2 Whisk the egg whites until stiff and slowly whisk in the sugar. Fold the two mixtures together with the chopped nuts and freeze. This ice cream can be served straight from the freezer.

Country Friends

Northleach
Chefs/proprietors *Charles and Pauline Whittaker*

Mushrooms and Bacon with Brandy and Cream

Serves 4

½ lb. (225g.) bacon, chopped
1 oz. (25g.) butter
1 lb. (450g.) button mushrooms
1 clove garlic, chopped
salt and black pepper
brandy
¾ pint (425ml.) double cream
Parmesan cheese

1 Fry the bacon in butter with the garlic. Add the mushrooms and toss well. Add the seasoning.

2 Add some brandy and flame. Remove mushrooms and bacon. Add the cream to the pan and boil rapidly until reduced by half.

Return mushrooms and bacon to pan and continue to boil rapidly until cream is thick.

3 Transfer to ramekin dishes and sprinkle with Parmesan. Brown in oven and serve.

Venison in a Blackcurrant Sauce

Serves 8

8 lb. (3¼ kilos) saddle venison, boned

For the marinade:
1 onion, sliced and lightly fried in butter
2 carrots, chopped and lightly fried in butter
1 bottle red wine
fresh parsley
garlic, crushed
6 black peppercorns

For the sauce:
8 tablespoons blackcurrants
¼ pint (150ml.) red wine vinegar
1 pint (575ml.) double cream
8 slices bread, soaked in 4 oz. (125g.) melted butter
blackcurrant jam
chopped parsley
2 oz. (50g.) butter
onion, carrot and celery for a stock

1 Soak the blackcurrants in the vinegar for at least a week before required.

2 Mix the marinade ingredients together.

3 Cut out the eye of the saddle in one long piece from each side. Trim all sinew off. The prepared meat should resemble a fillet of beef. Cut each strip into 4 portions and place in the marinade for at least 3 days.

4 Brown all the remaining meat trimmings and bones along with the onion, carrot and celery. Add 8 pints (4½ litres) of water and simmer for 5 hours. Strain and cool.

5 Cut 8 oval pieces from the bread. Lightly brown in a moderate oven. Spread with the jam and sprinkle with chopped parsley. Keep warm.

6 Lightly fry the venison in butter to seal. Place in a moderate oven and cook to order. Drain all the butter from the pan and add 1 pint (575ml.) stock and reduce by half. Add the blackcurrants with 2 tablespoons of the vinegar. Add cream and boil rapidly till thick. Place the venison on the croûtes and pour the sauce over.

Autumn Pudding

Serves 6

2½ lb. (generous kilo) prepared
    seasonal fruit e.g. apples, plums,
    blackberries, blueberries etc.
4 tablespoons water
2 oz. (50g.) soft brown sugar
8 thin slices brown bread

1 Stew the fruit gently with the water and sugar, starting with the apples and plums and only adding the berries at the last minute.

2 Remove the crusts from the bread and line a 2 lb. (900g.) pudding basin. Add most of the fruit and cover with the bread. Cover with tin foil and then a well fitting plate and a weight to press down. Leave overnight.

3 Strain the remaining fruit and boil juices rapidly till thick. Add fruit.

4 Turn the pudding out and top with the fruit.

Crane's

Salisbury
Chef/proprietor *Tom Geary*

Foie de Volaille en Cassolette

Serves 4

½ lb. (225g.) whole chicken livers,
 soaked in milk for 30 minutes
2 - 3 fl. oz. (50 - 75ml.) red wine
2 - 3 fl. oz. (50 - 75ml.) chicken stock
2 - 3 fl. oz. (50 - 75ml.) double cream
butter as necessary
1 oz. (25g.) clarified butter to cook
truffle for garnish

For the pâté brisée:
4 oz. (125g.) plain flour
2 oz. (50g.) butter
1 egg yolk
salt
iced water

1 Prepare the pâté brisée. Blind bake in individual, fluted tart cases.

2 Dry the livers and stiffen quickly in clarified butter. Remove from the pan and keep warm.

3 Pour away the butter and deglaze the pan with red wine. Reduce. Add the chicken stock and reduce again. Add the double cream and bring to the boil. Thicken more with butter.

4 Put chicken livers into tart cases, cover with sauce and garnish with truffle. Serve.

Fricasée de Ris au Rognons de Veau

Serves 4

1 pair fresh calf's sweetbreads
1 calf's kidney
2 oz. (50g.) clarified butter
seasoned flour

2 shallots, finely chopped
1 fl. oz. (25ml.) Cognac
2 - 3 fl. oz. (50 - 75ml.) white veal stock
2 - 3 oz. (50 - 75g.) fresh white
    mushrooms, sliced
2 - 3 fl. oz. (50 - 75ml.) double cream

1 Prepare and blanch the sweetbreads.

2 Skin and cut out core of kidney. Separate kidney nodes individually.

3 Heat the clarified butter in a sauté pan and stiffen the kidneys quickly on both sides — on no account overcook as calves' kidneys should be done to a rare condition. Remove and keep warm between two large dinner plates.

4 Dust the sweetbreads in seasoned flour and sauté gently until cooked. Remove and keep warm. Sweat the shallots in the juices in the pan and deglaze with Cognac. Add the veal stock, mushrooms and reduce. Add double cream and boil to thicken.

5 Return the kidneys and sweetbreads to the sauce in the pan and reheat gently. Serve with saffron rice garnished with petit pois.

Meringue Royale

mincemeat, enough to fill 9 - 10″ (23 - 26 cm.) flan case

For the meringue:
6 egg whites
¾ lb. (350g.) caster sugar

For the pâté brisée:
½ lb. (225g.) plain flour
¼ lb. (125g.) butter
2 egg yolks
salt
iced water

1 Prepare the pâté brisée and line the flan case. Bake blind.

2 Prepare a meringue with the egg whites and caster sugar.

3 Fill your flan case with mincemeat, top with meringue and bake in a moderate oven until meringue is browned to your liking. Serve with fresh cream.

Danielle

Limpley Stoke
Chef/proprietor *Ned Carlton Smith*

Salade Bourguignonne

Serves 4

For the salade:
1 head cos lettuce
½ lb. (225g.) haricots vert, blanched
4 branches celery
1 tablespoon parsley, chopped

For the dressing:
1 tablespoon butter
4 oz. (125g.) chicken livers
2 egg yolks
6 fl. oz. (175ml.) peanut or walnut oil
1 tablespoon wine vinegar
1 teaspoon Dijon mustard
salt and pepper

If you happen to have a tin of good foie gras in the fridge, just open it up, slice thinly and serve with a julienne of carrots and celery, cooked 'al dente' in walnut oil. If you find foie gras a little too rich, try the above.

1 Melt the butter in a saucepan. When foam begins to subside, add chicken livers and sauté over high heat quickly until browned on the outside and pink inside.

2 Remove from pan and season with salt and pepper. Allow to cool and roughly chop.

3 Put mustard into a mixing bowl and mix in wine vinegar. Then beat in the egg yolks, salt and pepper and lastly the oil, drop by drop.

4 Add the chicken livers and mix thoroughly. Serve garnished with parsley on chilled salad plates on a bed of lettuce, celery and haricots vert.

Rôti de Porc Danielle

4 lb. (1¾ kilos) loin pork, boned and skinned

For the marinade:
½ pint (275ml.) olive or peanut oil
juice 2 lemons
2 cloves garlic, finely crushed
2 tablespoons green peppercorns or 1 tablespoon black, crushed
5 - 6 branches thyme or ½ teaspoon dried
1 branch fresh rosemary
salt and pepper

For the sauce:
2 tablespoons Dijon mustard
½ pint (275ml.) double cream
½ pint (275ml.) white wine vinegar or cider vinegar
½ pint (275ml.) white wine
½ pint (275ml.) chicken stock
1 teaspoon green peppercorns
juice ½ lemon

Pork can often be dry and tasteless, unless treated carefully. Here it is the marinade that sets off the light flavour of the meat.

1 Rub the pork all over with salt and pepper, then turn the meat fat side down and rub in the garlic, thyme, rosemary and green peppercorns, until the meat is covered with the paste, meat side only. Reverse the meat and cover with the oil and lemon juice. Cover and put in a cool place and leave for 4 - 6 hours or overnight in the fridge.

2 Before cooking, roll and tie neatly. Roast in a hot oven for 30 minutes, turning at least twice. Reduce to 180°C/350°F/gas 4 and cook for another 60 minutes or until cooked, the meat juices should be golden when the meat is pricked. Remove to serving plate and keep warm.

3 While meat is cooking, boil down vinegar and white wine until reduced to one-third. Add double cream to the mustard by droplets until thoroughly mixed. Add the vinegar/wine mixture a few drops at a time, whisking vigorously. When completely mixed, set aside.

4 Pour off all but a spoonful of the fat from the roasting pan. Add 1 tablespoon flour and mix thoroughly. Add chicken stock and thoroughly mix till no lumps. Pass through a fine sieve, and add to the wine/vinegar mixture. Heat thoroughly. Just before serving add the lemon juice and green peppercorns. Pour over sliced pork and serve.

La Tarte Tatin

3 lb. (1½ kilos) apples, peeled, cored
   and sliced
7 oz. (200g.) caster sugar
½ lb. (225g.) unsalted butter
rind 1 lemon
sugar to sprinkle
flaky pastry
3½ fl. oz. (100ml.) water

Legend has it that one of the sisters Tatin (who ran a restaurant in France before World War 2) dropped a French apple tart while removing it from the oven. She picked it up, upside down, caramelised it and served it to customers who were delighted. We don't do ours that way.

1 Put about ¼ of the apple slices in a large frying pan, where you have melted about 2 tablespoons of the butter. Sprinkle generously with sugar and sauté until golden and tender but not crumbly. Transfer to a dish or bowl and continue until you have cooked all the apples. Don't try to cook too many at a time as they will crumble.

2 Grate the lemon on the apples and mix carefully but thoroughly.

3 While the apples are cooling, prepare the caramel. Boil the sugar in the water. Boil until mixture turns a rich caramel colour. Pour into a 9'' (23cm.) pyrex, round baking dish, covering the sides and bottom carefully and completely.

4 Arrange apple slices in flower pattern on the bottom of the dish and then line sides. Finally fill dish with remainder of apples. Cover dish with the rolled out pastry. Brush with egg yolks and prick to permit steam to escape.

5 Bake in pre-heated oven 190°C/375°F/gas 5 for about 30 minutes. Remove from oven and use a sharp knife to cut pastry all around edge. Put a 12'' (30cm.) plate on top of tarte and using 2 oven gloves, flip it over so that pastry is on bottom. The pyrex dish should come away cleanly — if it sticks pop whole thing in a very hot oven for about 5 minutes before another attempt.

Eethuys

West Stoughton
Chef/proprietor *Karen Roozen*

Indonesian Style Spare Ribs
Serves 4

2 lb. (900g.) spare ribs
oil and butter to cook
1 large onion
2 large cloves garlic
½ teaspoon each of coriander, cumin
   and ginger powder
¼ teaspoon turmeric
sweet Indonesian soy sauce or failing
   that, Hoi Sin sauce
6 candle nuts or any other nut
root or stem ginger

1 Fry the spare ribs in a mixture of oil and butter until brown.

2 Liquidise or chop extremely finely all the other ingredients, except for the soy sauce. Fry this mixture in oil and then add enough soy sauce to make a good sauce. Add the spare ribs and cook on a very low heat, covered, for about 1 hour. If the sauce is too thick, thin with some chicken stock. If liked, add bits of root ginger or stem ginger.

Osso Bucco à l'Orange
Serves 4

8 slices shin of veal, 1½'' (4 cm.) thick
flour
pepper
oil and butter to fry
1 clove garlic, finely chopped
1 large onion, finely chopped
stock
white wine
1 lb. (450g.) tomatoes, peeled and
   roughly chopped
tomato purée, to taste
rind of 1 orange and the juice
parsley, chopped

1 Flour and season the veal and brown in the oil and butter. Add the onion, garlic, tomatoes, 2 tablespoons purée and enough stock and wine to cover. Simmer on top of the oven, covered. After 1 hour, add the orange rind and juice and the chopped parsley.

2 Check from time to time to see if the meat is really tender. When done, allow to cool and degrease.

3 Heat through before serving. Accompany with rice.

Almond Cream

For the praline:
3 oz. (75g.) caster sugar
2 tablespoons water
3 oz. (75g.) flaked almonds

4 eggs, separated
3 oz. (75g.) caster sugar
1 oz. (25g.) flour
1 pint (575ml.) milk
almond essence
sponge cake
Amoretto liquour

1 Make the praline by boiling the sugar with a little water until caramel. Add the almond flakes and spoon out on to a buttered baking tray. When cold and set, take to it with a hammer or use a nut grinder or liquidiser. The latter makes it too fine I find and therefore not so successful.

2 Make the almond cream by whisking the 4 egg yolks with the sugar until lemon coloured. Add the flour and beat in well. Boil the milk and add gently to the yolks. Boil up the mixture very gently over a low heat. Add a few drops of almond essence. Fold in some of the praline.

3 Make individual portions by arranging some sponge cake in the bottom of a glass. Sprinkle with Amoretto and spoon over the custard. Just before serving, cover the top with crunchy praline.

Flowers

Bath
Chef/proprietor *Teresa Lipin*

Avocado and Spinach Salad with Hot Bacon

Serves 6

¼ lb. (125g.) spinach leaves
¼ lb. (125g.) button mushrooms, sliced
3 ripe avocados, sliced
¼ lb. (125g.) smoked streaky bacon,
   sliced

For the French dressing:
1 tablespoon French mustard,
   preferably with seeds
1 teaspoon caster sugar
4 tablespoons olive or corn oil
1 tablespoon wine vinegar
salt and pepper to taste

1 Wash the spinach leaves and shred finely.

2 Cook the bacon until crisp.

3 Arrange the spinach leaves and mushrooms on individual plates or bowls with the avocado in the centre. Pour the vinaigrette dressing over and then top with hot bacon and a little of the bacon fat. Serve immediately.

Sea Bream in Red Wine with Garlic and Tomato Sauce

Serves 6

12 fillets sea bream
⅓ bottle red wine

For the sauce:
2 lb. (900g.) ripe tomatoes, roughly
   chopped and cored
1 can tomato juice

2 cloves garlic, finely chopped
¼ pint (150ml.) corn oil
chopped parsley or chives to garnish

1 Skin the fish and place in an earthenware
dish. Pour the wine over and cover dish with
foil or greaseproof paper. Place in a
preheated oven 190°C/375°F/gas 5 for
about 15 minutes or until cooked.

2 Heat the oil in a pan and sauté the garlic.
Add the tomatoes and when soft add the
tomato juice. Season to taste.

3 To serve, place 2 fillets of bream onto
each plate with a little juice from the dish and
then spoon the tomato sauce on top.
Sprinkle with chopped parsley or chives.

Steamed Chocolate Pudding

Serves 6

5 oz. (150g.) bitter chocolate
7½ oz. (210g.) fresh white breadcrumbs
3 oz. (75g.) butter
3 oz. (75g.) caster sugar
7 fl. oz. (200ml.) milk
3 eggs
few drops vanilla essence
pinch cinnamon

1 Cut the chocolate into small pieces and
dissolve slowly in the milk.

2 Cream the butter in a basin and sieve the
sugar on top. Add the yolks and few of the
breadcrumbs and mix well. Then add the
chocolate, vanilla essence, cinnamon and
the rest of the crumbs. Mix again.

3 Whip the egg whites to a stiff froth and fold
lightly into the rest of the mixture. Pour the
mixture into a well greased mould and cover
with greased paper. Place the mould in a
large saucepan with about 1″ (2.5cm.) of
water in it and steam the pudding, semi-
covered, gently for about 1 hour or until it has
risen and feels firm to the touch. Serve with
thick cream.

Harveys

Bristol
Chef *Andy Hunt*

Soupe de Poissons Moderne

Serves 4

2 pints (generous litre) fish stock
1 lb. (450g.) mixed fish, whiting, red
   mullet, conger eel, John Dory,
crayfish and mussels, in shell
4 fl. oz. (125ml.) dry white wine
4 oz. (125g.) potatoes, roughly diced
½ lb. (225g.) tomatoes, roughly
   chopped
1 oz. (25g.) tomato purée
2 oz. (50g.) onion and white of leek,
   roughly chopped
1 fl. oz. (25ml.) oil
bouquet garni
2 cloves garlic, crushed
pinch saffron
salt to season and ground black pepper
Gruyère, grated
8 croûtes of French bread, toasted

For the garlic dressing:
2 fl. oz. (50ml.) egg yolks
2 cloves garlic, crushed
pinch saffron
salt and black pepper
squeeze lemon juice
4 fl. oz. (125g.) oil

1 Heat oil in a thick bottomed saucepan and add the onion, leek and garlic and sweat gently until softened. Add the fish and purée and continue to cook gently for 5 minutes.

2 Stir in the wine, fish stock, bring to the boil and skim. Add the potato, tomatoes, bouquet garni, saffron and seasoning. Simmer gently for approximately 30 - 45 minutes. Remove bouquet garni and pass the soup into a clean saucepan, reheat and correct seasoning.

3 Make the garlic dressing by whisking the egg yolk, garlic, saffron, lemon juice and seasoning. Whisk in the oil gradually, as if making mayonnaise, to form an emulsified garlic dressing. Spread the toasted croûtes with the dressing and sprinkle with the cheese. To serve, ladle the soup into dishes and garnish with croûtes and chopped parsley.

Rognons de Veau Bordelaise

2 large veal kidneys
4 oz. (125g.) beef marrow, gently
    poached for 5 minutes in salt water
6 oz. (175g.) onions, finely chopped
¼ pint (150ml.) red wine
freshly milled peppercorns
butter
pinch salt
pinch fresh thyme
bayleaf
¼ pint (150ml.) demi-glacé (refined
    brown sauce)

1 Slice the kidneys in thin escalopes and remove sinews. Sauté quickly in a little oil to seal. Remove kidneys and keep warm. Discard residue.

2 Add a good 1 oz. (25g.) butter to the pan and quickly sauté the onions. Deglaze with the red wine and add the milled peppercorns and aromates and reduce by half. Add the demi-glacé and simmer for 20 minutes. Pass through a fine strainer.

3 Arrange kidneys on a serving dish, place the beef marrow on top and coat with the Bordelaise sauce. Finish with chopped parsley.

Soufflé Grand Marnier

2 oz. (50g.) butter
2 oz. (50g.) flour
3 oz. (75g.) caster sugar
½ pint (275ml.) milk
1 vanilla pod
4 eggs yolks
6 egg whites, stiffly beaten to snow
1 sherry glass (copita) Grand Marnier

The secret of a good soufflé is constant heat. Do not put the soufflé into a very hot oven first to make it rise and then reduce the heat. This is often the reason why so many people fail in making soufflés.

1 Butter and sugar a 4/5'' (10/13cm.) soufflé dish and surround the dish with greased and sugared greaseproof paper.

2 Melt the butter and add flour. Cook out gently with no colour. Add the milk slowly with the vanilla pod and sugar. Bring to the boil and remove the vanilla pod. Cool slightly and beat in the egg yolks and the Grand Marnier. Fold in the stiffly beaten egg whites. Pour very carefully into the soufflé dish, up to two-thirds of its depth.

3 Bake for 20 minutes in a moderate oven. Serve immediately.

The Hole in the Wall

Bath
Chefs/proprietors *Sue and Tim Cumming*

Crab en Cocotte with Port and a Cheese Sauce

Serves 6

meat from 2 crabs or 1 lb. (450g.) crab
    meat
4 oz. (125g.) mushrooms, sliced
1 oz. (25g.) butter
3 fl. oz. (75g.) port
2½ fl. oz. (60ml.) double cream
salt and pepper

For the sauce:
1 oz. (25g.) flour
1 oz. (25g.) butter
14 fl. oz. (400ml.) milk
Gruyère or Jarlsberg, grated

1 Soften the mushrooms in the butter. Add the port and reduce. Add the double cream, season and bring to the boil. Remove from heat. Divide the mixture between 6 cocotte dishes or the two crab shells. Put the crab meat on top.

2 Prepare a Béchamel sauce with the flour and butter and cook without browning. Add the heated milk slowly, stirring all the time until reduced.

3 Mask the crab meat with 2 or 3 tablespoons of the Béchamel, sprinkle with the cheese and bake in a hot oven for 15 minutes.

Pheasant, Marinaded and Cooked in Gigondas

Serves 4 - 6

2 pheasants, jointed
rashers smoked bacon
6 oz. (175g.) onions, cut into ½'' (1 cm.)
    pieces
6 oz. (175g.) carrots, cut into ½'' (1 cm.)
    pieces
⅓ bottle Gigondas
⅓ bottle Côtes du Rhone
bouquet garni, made from 1 clove and 1
    clove garlic
oil to fry
1 tablespoon flour
2 fl. oz. (50ml.) Crème de Cassis
1 tablespoon cream
24 little onions
fleurons and parsley to garnish

1 Wrap each pheasant joint in a rasher smoked bacon, pinned with a cocktail stick. Place in a bowl with the onions, carrots, wine and the bouquet garni. Allow to marinade for at least 6 hours.

2 Take the pheasant out of the marinade and fry in a little oil. Transfer to a casserole.

3 Take out the vegetables from the marinade and fry. Sprinkle with the flour, add the marinade liquid and make a sauce. Pour the sauce over the pheasant and cook in a low oven until tender.

4 When cooked take out the pheasant, remove cocktail sticks and keep warm. Strain the sauce, reheat and add the Crème de Cassis, cream and check seasoning. Pour over the pheasant.

5 Separately fry the little onions in oil until brown. Borrow some of the red wine sauce to braise the onions until they are 'al dente'. Serve the pheasant with the onions, fleurons and parsley.

Prune, Almond and Armagnac Tart

For the sweet pastry:
10 oz. (275g.) plain flour
7 oz. (200g.) butter
3 oz. (75g.) caster sugar
1 whole egg
1 egg yolk
pinch salt
2 oz. (50g.) ground almonds
grated rind ½ lemon
2 generous tablespoons rum

For the batter:
10 tablespoons whipping cream
4 whole eggs
8 tablespoons vanilla sugar
6 tablespoons ground almonds
4 tablespoons orange flower water
2 oz. (50g.) butter, melted

1 lb. (450g.) fresh prunes, stoned
redcurrant jelly
6 tablespoons Armagnac

1 Make the pastry by mixing together in a bowl or on a pastry board all the dry ingredients. Then cut the butter into cubes and put into a well in the centre of the flour along with the eggs and rum. Work lightly until completely mixed but do not overwork. Place in the refrigerator until needed. Preheat the oven to 200°C/400°F/gas 6.

2 Roll out the pastry and line a 10" (26cm.) flan dish. Prick the pastry with a fork and trim the edges of the pastry. Put the prunes in the flan dish and cover with a few tablespoons of the redcurrant jelly and put in oven for 10 - 15 minutes to start the cooking.

3 Whisk together all the batter ingredients, except the butter. When whisked, add the butter, still whisking.

4 After 10 - 15 minutes take the tart case out of the oven and cover with the batter and bake for another 25 minutes. When·cooked, sprinkle the tart with 6 tablespoons of Armagnac and serve warm.

Homewood Park

Hinton Charterhouse
Chef/proprietor *Stephen Ross*

Potted Salmon and Sole

Serves 4

¾ lb. (350g.) salmon
4 fillets or ¾ lb. (350g.) sole
1 lemon segment
white wine or cider to poach
1 teaspoon dill
pinch nutmeg
1 teaspoon parsley, freshly chopped
2 eggs, hardboiled and finely chopped
salt and pepper
clarified butter

1 Poach the sole and salmon with a little lemon in the white wine or cider. Allow to cool.

2 Flake the fish into a suitable bowl — so that the fish virtually fills it. Cover with the egg, lemon segment and seasonings.

3 Chill and cover with clarified butter. Serve with toast and perhaps a cucumber salad.

Fillet of Roe Deer with Sour Cream and Capers

Serves 6

1 small haunch roe deer
1 small onion, finely chopped
1 rasher streaky bacon, finely chopped
¼ pint (150ml.) white wine
¼ pint (150ml.) chicken stock
grated rind and juice of 2 lemons
½ pint (275ml.) sour cream
handful capers
butter for frying

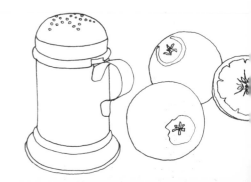

1 Cut 12 ¼ " (1 cm.) thick escalopes of venison from your haunch — this will be most of the haunch.

2 In a sauté pan, quickly fry the escalopes in very hot butter. Remove to a serving dish and keep warm.

3 To the same pan, add the onion and bacon, white wine and chicken stock. Reduce by half. Add the lemon juice, rind, soured cream and capers. Check seasoning. Pour the sauce over the escalopes and serve with rice or new potatoes.

Mrs. Siddons Cake

¾ lb. (350g.) rich short crust pastry
1½ lb. (675g.) 1st grade dried apricots,
    soaked overnight
¾ lb. (350g.) marzipan
3 oz. (75g.) sultanas
grated rind 1 lemon
cinnamon and nutmeg
½ lb. (250g.) caster sugar
brandy

1 Poach the apricots in the brandy and caster sugar until soft. About 15 - 20 minutes.

2 Line a loose bottomed cake tin with two-thirds of the pastry. Chill.

3 Drain the apricots and cover the bottom of the tin. Break up the marzipan into small pieces and dot over the apricots. Sprinkle in some sultanas, cinnamon, nutmeg and lemon rind. Repeat until the tin is full.

4 Put the remaining pastry on top, flute the edges and decorate. Glaze with egg yolk and sprinkle with caster sugar. Put into oven and cook until the top of the cake is done. Take out of oven and remove the sides of the tin. Glaze the sides of the cake, cover the top and return to the oven to lightly brown. Leave in a warm place before serving. Serve warm.

Hunstrete House

Hunstrete
Chef *Alain Dubois*

Terrine of Ham and Vegetables with a Fresh Tomato Sauce

Serves 6

12 oz. (350g.) cooked ham
4 egg whites
selection of vegetables:
   4 oz. (125g.) carrots, chopped
   4 oz. (125g.) asparagus, chopped
   4 oz. (125g.) artichoke, chopped
   4 oz. (125g.) French beans, chopped
¼ pint (150ml.) olive oil
¼ pint (150ml.) double cream

For the tomato sauce:
2 large onions, chopped
2 carrots, chopped
1½ lb. (875g.) fresh tomatoes, roughly
   chopped
1 tablespoon basil, freshly chopped
2 cloves garlic, chopped
1 pint (575ml.) chicken or vegetable
   stock
1 dessertspoon tomato purée
salt and pepper

1 Prepare and blanch your vegetables.

2 Make a mousse of the ham by liquidising along with the egg whites. Put over ice and beat in the oil and cream. Add a pinch of salt.

3 Well grease a terrine and put a small amount of the mousse in the bottom and then a layer of vegetables, continue like this until the terrine is full. Cover and bake in a bain marie at 180°C/350°F/gas 4 for 35 minutes.

4 To make the tomato sauce, sweat the onion, garlic and carrot. Add the tomatoes, and the purée, stock and basil. Boil rapidly for about 30 minutes until tender. Liquidise and pass through a fine sieve. Serve to accompany the terrine.

Breast of Duck with Madeira Sauce

Serves 4

4 duck breasts
fine julienne of celery, carrots and leeks
1 glass Madeira
2 glasses stock
¼ pint (150ml.) double cream
Grand Marnier
unsalted butter
watercress

1 Mark the fat on the duck breasts.

2 Cook the julienne of vegetables in a little butter, flame with Grand Marnier and add the cream. Reduce by two-thirds and keep in a warm place.

3 Season the duck breasts and cook without any fat until pink. Discard the fat from the pan and deglaze with the Madeira. Reduce by two-thirds and add the stock, reduce again and finish with a small piece of unsalted butter to thicken the sauce.

4 Place the vegetable julienne on a plate and slice the duck breasts and arrange on top. Pour the Madeira sauce around the duck and garnish with a sprig of fresh watercress.

Chocolate Rum Pots

Serves 8

½ lb. (225g.) good quality plain dark
    chocolate
1 oz. (25g.) butter, salted
6 egg yolks
generous tot rum, to flavour
10 egg whites, stiffly beaten

This excellent sweet is very adaptable. You can easily substitute the rum with the spirit of your choice, perhaps Grand Marnier or mint liqueur.

1 Melt the chocolate and butter over a saucepan of hot water. Off the heat, beat in the egg yolks and the rum, keep whisking until the mixture thickens. Leave to cool and then fold in the stiffly beaten egg whites.

2 Finish with flaked chocolate over the top of the rum pots.

45

Keith Floyd's

Bristol
Chef/proprietor *Keith Floyd*

Terrine du Gibier
Serves 12

2 lb. (900g.) raw flesh, hare, pheasant,
    venison, grouse
some derinded bacon rashers
2 lb. (900g.) raw belly pork
1 lb. (450g.) fat bacon
3 glasses brandy
thyme and parsley
salt and pepper
bay leaves
2 whole eggs
1 cup double cream

It is preferable for the success of this terrine that you use all four game ingredients, but actually one will do. This terrine can be kept in the refrigerator for at least 2½ weeks.

1 Mince the pork, chop the fat bacon and very finely chop the game.

2 Mix the pork, game and fat bacon with the herbs, salt and pepper, cream, eggs and brandy. Fill a good sized terrine with the mixture and cover the top with bacon rashers and a bayleaf or two.

3 Cook in a bain marie in a slow oven for about 2 hours. Leave to cool for at least 12 hours before slicing thinly and eating with a glass of dry Madeira.

La Bourride
Serves 6

FIRST make a good fish bouillon
SECOND make a good aioli (you know, egg yolks, olive oil and garlic)
THIRD don't be a cheapskate buy some decent fish
By which I mean:
    one good white fish, monkfish or turbot — 2 lb. (900g.)
    3 crayfish or lobsters
    and if possible a whole bream or bass — 2 lb. (900g.)

La Bourride, is a Phoenician dish of some two thousand years standing. Which delighted the palates of gastronauts long before bouillabaise and 'super little meals' were discovered by anorak wearing, estate car driving hordes in the rip off restos of France.
The recipe I use in Keith Floyd's restaurant owes something to one of the better restaurants of Marseille, Michel.
In the Rue Catalan.
Which is nowhere near the Vieux Port.
Or is it?
But however you view food and its location you cannot escape the above requirements.

1 Now all you have to do is, having cleaned and prepared your fish, poach them lightly in the fish bouillon.

2 Then put them on a serving plate. Now over a low heat, stir in the aioli to about ½ of the bouillon until it thickens like custard and pour it over the fish.

3 You can save some of the aioli to serve separately with the dish. And you can make croûtons too. And of course you should read the whole recipe before you attempt the dish. And this might involve you in finding out how to make bouillon and aioli.

Chocolate Galette

Serves 8 - 10

For the pastry:
7 oz. (200g.) plain flour
1 oz. (25g.) cocoa powder
5 oz. (150g.) butter
3 oz. (75g.) icing sugar
3 egg yolks, beaten

For the filling:
½ lb. (225g.) butter
1 measure brandy
3 oz. (75g.) cocoa powder
2 oz. (50g.) icing sugar

For the covering:
1 block expensive dark chocolate
1 oz. (25g.) butter
4 tablespoons milk

1 Make the pastry by mixing the cocoa, flour and icing sugar together. Add the beaten eggs and knead in the butter. Leave to rest for 1 hour before rolling out. Divide into three 10" (26 cm.) rounds about 1/8" (.3 cm.) thick — in other words, as thin as possible. Bake for 5 or 6 minutes at 200°C/400°F/gas 6. Leave to cool.

2 Now mix the filling ingredients together to make a rich chocolate butter cream. Spread the cream over the round to make a three-tiered sandwich. By now the whole thing is about ¾" (1.5 cm.) in height.

3 Finally melt the dark chocolate with the butter and the milk and pour over the galette. If you like you could grate some hard chocolate over the whole thing when the top has set.

Kings Arms

Chipping Camden
Chef/proprietor *Rosemary Willmott*

Stuffed Mushrooms en Coquille

Serves 4

¾ lb. (350g.) cup mushrooms
small bunch freshly chopped chives and
    parsley
4 tablespoons breadcrumbs
2 egg yolks
2 - 3 tablespoons double cream
1 clove garlic, chopped
seasoning

1 De-stalk the mushrooms. Chop the stalks
with a few extra mushrooms. Add the herbs,
breadcrumbs and bind with the egg yolks,
cream and garlic. Add seasoning.

2 Stuff the mushrooms with the mixture and
top with a creamy cheese sauce. Bake in a
hot oven until a delicious golden brown.

Salmon and Smoked Salmon Quenelles with Béarnaise Sauce

Serves 4

¾ lb. (350g.) raw fresh salmon
¼ lb. (125g.) smoked salmon
2 grated lemon rinds
anchovy essence
¼ pint (150ml.) double cream
ground black pepper
white wine and fish stock for poaching

For the choux paste:
4 oz. (125g.) flour
½ pint (275ml.) water
2 oz. (50g.) butter
2 whole eggs
2 egg whites

For the Béarnaise sauce:
3 egg yolks
½ lb. (225g.) unsalted butter
2 fl. oz. (50ml.) wine vinegar
6 peppercorns
2 bayleaves
tarragon and parsley, freshly chopped

1 Blend the fish until smooth. Add seasonings, lemon rind and double cream. Chill.

2 Make the choux paste and cool. When cool, add the salmon mixture and make into quenelles. Poach in white wine and stock for 3 - 4 minutes and serve with the Béarnaise sauce.

3 To make the sauce, whisk the egg yolks over hot water until thick. Add the melted butter slowly, whisking all the while. Make a reduction from the wine vinegar, peppercorns and bayleaves. Strain. Whisk into the egg and butter mix and season. Finally add some chopped tarragon and parsley.

Hot Bananas, Rum and Cream   *Serves 4*

2 large bananas
2 tablespoons dark rum
unsalted butter
1 tablespoon dark brown sugar
double cream

1 Slice the bananas lengthwise. Toss in unsalted butter until soft. Flame with the rum, add the cream and top with brown sugar.

2 Pop under a hot grill and serve.

Langley House

Langley Marsh
Chef/proprietor *Rosalind McCulloch*

Fresh Peaches with Herb and Cheese Pâté

Serves 6

6 peaches, halved and stoned
orange slices and walnuts to decorate

For the pâté:
1 lb. (450g.) cream cheese
6 oz. (175g.) butter
4 cloves garlic
1 tablespoon each of dried chervil,
    chopped parsley, thyme and any
    other herb you might fancy
seasoning

1 Melt the butter very gently.

2 Put all the other ingredients into a beater and blend slowly together, frequently stopping to clear the blade. As the mixture is beginning to come together, still beating, slowly and gently pour in the melted butter. If this is not done very slowly the mixture can curdle.

3 To serve, place the halved peach on a daintily prepared salad of lettuce, oranges and walnuts and pipe rosettes of the pâté into the centre of the peach and top with a whole walnut.

Filet de Porc en Croûte

Serves 4 - 6

½ lb. (225g.) puff pastry
1 large pork tenderloin
3 oz. (75g.) butter
1 large onion, finely chopped
1 glove garlic, chopped
¼ lb. (125g.) mushrooms, chopped
¼ lb. (125g.) cooked ham, finely
    shredded
Herbes de Provence (dried, mixed
    Provençal herbs)
fresh parsley and sage
salt and black pepper

1 Remove any skin and fat from the pork. Cut in two lengthways. Place one piece between tin foil and beat with a rolling pin until 2" (5 cm.) wide and about 14" (34 cm.) long. Trim the sides straight. Gently heat 1 oz. (25g.) of the butter in a large frying pan and fry the first piece of tenderloin until slightly coloured. Remove and leave to cool. Repeat with the second piece of pork.

2 Fry the chopped onion, garlic and mushrooms in the remaining butter until soft. Add the dried herbs and seasoning and cook for 3 minutes. Turn into a bowl and add the fresh herbs and ham. Leave to cool.

3 Roll out the pastry to a rectangle. Divide into two with one piece two-thirds larger than the other. Place the larger piece on a baking tray and lay one tenderloin in the middle and cover with half of the stuffing. Repeat and press the pastry around the sides. Lay the remaining pastry on top — you can chill until needed at this stage.

4 When required, brush with egg glaze and decorate with fleurons. Bake in a hot oven for 35 to 40 minutes or until nicely browned. If liked you may serve hot or cold with a Sauce Chasseur.

Wine and Brandy Syllabub

Serves 6

½ pint (275ml.) double cream
4 fl. oz. (125ml.) white wine
1 fl. oz. (25ml.) brandy
juice 1 lemon
3 oz. (75g.) caster sugar

1 Place the wine, brandy, sugar and lemon juice in a bowl and beat with an electric hand mixer on speed 2.

2 Very slowly add the double cream in a slow stream, beating all the time, until the mixture forms soft peaks. Carefully continue beating until the mixture is stiff. Spoon into glasses and serve. If you want you can freeze this syllabub.

Loaves and Fishes

Rockley
Chef/proprietor *Angela Rawson*

Stilton Doughnuts with a Stilton Sauce

Serves 6

8 oz. (225g.) plain flour
salt and black pepper
½ level teaspoon of bicarbonate of soda
1 oz. (25g.) unsalted butter
1 large egg
4 oz. (125g.) Stilton
little milk
1 level teaspoon Cream of Tatar

For the Stilton sauce:
4 oz. (125g.) Stilton
¼ pint (150ml.) single cream
salt and pepper

1 Sift the flour, bicarbonate of soda, Cream of Tatar, salt and pepper together.

2 In a bowl, crumble the Stilton and chop the butter into small pieces. Cream these two together until smooth. Rub this mixture into the rest of the dry ingredients.

3 Beat the egg with 3 tablespoons of milk and blend with the cheese mixture. The dough must be fairly soft but holding its shape. Add a little more milk if needed.

4 Deep fry, in teaspoon amounts, in very hot oil until golden brown and crisp. You may have to turn the doughnuts half way through cooking. Serve at once accompanied with the Stilton sauce.

5 To make the Stilton sauce, simply liquidise the Stilton and cream together. Add seasoning.

Lamb Fillet en Croûte with Shrewsbury Sauce

Serves 4

4 lamb fillets, cut from the leg of a lamb
    1″ (2 cm.) thick
½ lb. (225g.) puff pastry
1 beaten egg
2 oz. unsalted butter

For the Shrewsbury sauce:
1 carrot, chopped into dice
1 onion, chopped into dice
2 sticks celery, chopped into dice
2 oz. (50g.) good dripping
1 sprig rosemary, thyme and parsley
    tied together

1 tablespoon plain flour
3 tablespoons redcurrant jelly
lamb trimmings
½ pint (275ml.) red wine
1 pint (575ml.) brown stock
1 dessertspoon tomato purée

1 Fry the lamb fillets on both sides in the butter to seal. Season. Place to one side and allow to cool completely.

2 Roll out the pastry into 4 squares and put the lamb fillets on each. Moisten the edges with beaten egg and fold over to make cases. Make a small hole in the top of each. Decorate with pastry leaves, cover and put to rest in the refrigerator until required. Preheat the oven to 220°C/425°F/gas 7, brush the cases with beaten egg and cook for 30 minutes until golden brown. Serve with the Shrewsbury sauce.

3 Fry the vegetables in the dripping until they absorb the fat. Stir in the flour and cook, stirring all the time until they become a nice brown colour. Take off the heat and whisk in wine, stock, purée, trimmings, herbs and seasoning. Return to a low heat and simmer very slowly for 2 hours. Strain the sauce. Just before serving, add the redcurrant jelly and heat through.

Honey and Lime Soufflé

3 large eggs, separated
2 dessertspoons clear honey
3 oz. (75g.) caster sugar
3 tablespoons water
3 limes
juice 1 small lemon
3 teaspoons gelatine
½ pint (275ml.) whipping cream

1 Prepare a 5"(13 cm.) soufflé dish. Tie a band of double thickness greaseproof paper firmly around the dish. Make the band 3" (8 cm.) taller than the dish.

2 Whisk the egg yolks with the caster sugar and honey until very thick and mousse like. Grate the rind of 2 limes and add to the egg mixture. Mix in the juice of the 2 limes and the lemon and whisk until thick.

3 Dissolve the gelatine in the water and pour into the soufflé mixture in a steady flow.

4 Whip half the cream, retaining the rest for decoration. Whisk the egg whites until stiff but not dry. With a large metal spoon, fold the whipped cream evenly into the soufflé mixture turning the bowl as you do so. Now add ⅓ of the egg whites, folding in very carefully. Add the rest of the egg whites. Do not over mix.

5 Pour the mixture into the soufflé dish, allowing it to come above the rim of the dish. Put into refrigerator to chill and set. Decorate with the rest of the whipped cream and slices of fresh lime.

Michael's

Bristol
Chef/proprietor *Michael McGowan*

Smoked Salmon and Avocado Roulade

Serves 6

For the roulade:
½ lb. (225g.) fresh salmon, skinned and boned
½ lb. (225g.) smoked salmon pieces
scant ½ pint (275ml.) milk
3 eggs, separated
1 teaspoon salt
1 fl. oz. (25ml.) dry sherry

For the avocado mousse:
4 small ripe avocados
1 teaspoon salt
½ pint (275ml.) mayonnaise
¼ pint (150ml.) double cream
¼ pint (150ml.) white wine
3 level teaspoons gelatine

1 For the roulade, blend the fresh salmon and sherry in a food processor. Add the egg yolks, milk and salt. Blend again until smooth. Transfer the mixture to a large bowl.

2 In a separate bowl, whisk the egg whites until stiff. Add one-third of the stiffened egg whites to the salmon and mix thoroughly. Then fold in the rest carefully. Line a flat baking tray with oiled greaseproof paper and spread on the mixture. Bake at 180°C/350°F/gas 4 for 15 - 20 minutes. Leave to cool. Blend the smoked salmon and spread onto the roulade.

3 For the mousse, dissolve the gelatine in the white wine over a gentle heat. Blend the avocados, then add the salt, mayonnaise, cream, wine and gelatine. Blend again until very smooth. Refrigerate.

4 When the mousse has very nearly set, spread on top of the roulade and carefully roll up. Refrigerate for at least 1 hour before serving.

Fillet Steak with Red Pepper Butter and Watercress Purée

Serves 6 - 8

4 - 6 oz. (125 - 175g.) fillet steak per person

For the watercress purée:
4 bunches watercress
pinch nutmeg
½ teaspoon salt
¼ pint (150ml.) double cream

For the sauce:
4 large red peppers, seeded and chopped
2 tablespoons oil
1 small onion, chopped
juice 1 lemon
1 lb. (450g.) butter, softened
salt and white pepper

1 Make the purée by plunging the watercress in a pan of boiling water for 10 seconds and refresh immediately in cold running water. Drain. Remove the thick parts of the stalks and place leaves into a blender with the seasoning. Boil the cream, add to the watercress and blend.

2 To make the sauce, stir the peppers in hot oil for 5 minutes. Reduce the heat and cover for a further 15 minutes. In a separate pan, sauté the onions until transparent. Place the hot peppers, onions, juice of the lemon and little white pepper into the blender. Gradually add the softened butter, blending all the while. Correct seasoning.

3 To finish the dish, cut the fillet steak into slices, barely ¼ " (.5cm.) thick. Brush with oil and season with salt and pepper. Heat a heavy bottomed pan and cook the meat over a high heat for about 2 minutes on each side. Keep warm.

4 Place a mound of the purée on each plate. Surround with the red pepper sauce, which may be reheated but must not boil. Place the slices of meat overlapping on top of the sauce and serve.

Chocolate Praline Ice Cream

Serves 6

½ lb. (225g.) dark chocolate
6 tablespoons milk
1 teaspoon coffee essence or powder
1 pint (575ml.) double cream

For the custard:
5 egg yolks
5 oz. (150g.) caster sugar
pinch salt
1 pint (575ml.) single cream
2 teaspoons vanilla essence

For the praline:
2 oz. (50g.) peeled almonds
2 oz. (50g.) caster sugar

1 For the praline, place the almonds and sugar in a flat baking tray and bake or grill, turning frequently until the sugar has caramelised and the almonds have turned a golden brown. When cool, break up with a rolling pin.

2 Make the custard by whisking the egg yolks, salt and sugar in a clean saucepan until light and creamy. In a separate pan, bring the cream and vanilla to the boil. Off the heat, pour the boiling cream onto the eggs and sugar, stirring well as you go. Stir over a very low heat until the mixture thickens sufficiently to cover the back of a wooden spoon.

3 Dissolve the chocolate and coffee in the milk over a gentle heat. Add the double cream. Combine the mixture with the custard and cool.

4 Freeze the ice cream mixture, adding the praline to taste, just before the mixture sets. Reserve a little of the praline to sprinkle over the ice cream before serving. Best results will be obtained by using an ice cream churn. Alternatively place the mixture in the freezer and bring out from time to time and give a good stir.

Old Parsonage

Farrington Gurney
Chef/proprietor *H. M. Gofton-Watson*

Prawns and Mushrooms in White Wine and Cream with Garlic

Serves 6

¾ lb. (350g.) peeled prawns
½ lb. (225g.) button mushrooms,
    chopped
½ pint (275ml.) white sauce
2 tablespoons white wine
6 fl. oz. (175ml.) double cream
1 clove garlic, crushed
mixture Parmesan cheese and brown
    breadcrumbs

1 Fry the mushrooms in butter. Add the white sauce, wine and cream and blend together, cooking gently.

2 Add the prawns and garlic to taste and heat for a little while longer and check seasoning.

3 Place into 6 heatproof dishes and sprinkle with the Parmesan and breadcrumbs. Place under grill to finish off.

Noisettes of Lamb with Mixed Herb Butter

Serves 6

12 loin of lamb cutlets, boned and rolled
1 dessertspoon each of the following
    fresh herbs (dried freeze if out of
    season):
        parsley
        fennel
        chervil
        basil
        chives
        tarragon

1 clove garlic, crushed
lemon juice
salt and pepper
½ lb. (225g.) unsalted butter

1 Cream the butter and beat in the herbs and garlic. Add the lemon juice, salt and pepper to taste. Form into a roll, using old butter papers and refrigerate.

2 Grill the lamb cutlets. When cooked, place a round of butter on each cutlet and flash under grill.

Walnut Tart

Serves 6

sweet pastry to line 8″ (20 cm.) flan ring
2 oz. (50g.) ground almonds
4 oz. (125g.) light brown sugar
2 eggs, separated
2 oz. (50g.) chopped walnuts
1 tablespoon lemon juice
1 cup maple syrup

1 Cream the egg yolks with the sugar until white and fluffy. Beat in the ground almonds and add the walnuts.

2 Stiffly beat the egg whites and fold into the mixture. Add the maple syrup and lemon juice and mix well together.

3 Fill the lined flan ring and bake in the centre of a pre-heated oven at 200°C/400°F/ gas 6 for approximately 40 minutes.

4 When cooked, remove ring and place tart on a cooling tray. Serve with whipped cream and chopped walnuts.

The Priory

Bath
Chef *Mike Collom*

Melon Raj

Serves 4

2 ripe Ogen melons
2 breasts cooked chicken
¼ pint (150ml.) home made
   mayonnaise
pinch curry powder, to taste
4 oz. (125g.) black grapes
4 oz. (125g.) white grapes
sprig parsley
crushed ice

1 Cut the melons in half and remove pips.
Trim the base so that they sit flat.

2 Remove the skin from the chicken and cut
into ½" (1cm.) pieces. Place inside each
melon half, so that they are nearly full.

3 Mix the mayonnaise with the curry powder
to obtain a light but not too hot sauce. Coat
the chicken only with the sauce. NB. Do not
coat the chicken too early with the sauce,
however for a dinner party all the
preparation can be done in advance, simply
coat the melon 5 minutes before serving.
Decorate the edge of the melon with
alternate slices of green and black grapes
and place a sprig of parsley in the middle.
Serve on crushed ice.

Rosettes of Lamb with Basil Sauce

Serves 4

1 complete loin and best end of lamb,
   boned and rolled
4 sprigs fresh basil, finely chopped, or 1
   tablespoon dried
1 pint (575ml.) veal stock
½ pint (275ml.) double cream

2 tablespoons Madeira
2 oz. (50g.) butter
oil
4 tomatoes and 8 mint leaves for garnish
salt and pepper.

1 Tie the loin in such a way as to give you 16 rosettes — allow 1″ (2cm.) between each string. Cut through and place rosettes on a tray. Put to one side.

2 Prepare the garnish by peeling the tomatoes with a very sharp knife, as if peeling an apple. Do not break the spiral of tomato skin. Roll up to form a tomato rose and put to one side.

3 Season the rosettes and in a large frying pan, heat the butter and oil and quickly fry off the lamb. You will probably have to fry 8 first, take out and keep warm and repeat. Lamb is best kept pink, so do not overcook as the sauce takes a little time to prepare.

4 As soon as the last rosette is cooked, place the veal stock and basil in the pan, reduce by half and add the double cream and Madeira. Reduce again, check for seasoning and finish with a knob of butter. Keep warm.

5 On 4 hot dinner plates, arrange the rosettes of lamb, minus the string, in the middle. Place the tomato roses and mint in the centre and pour the sauce around the edge of the rosettes. Serve at once with a selection of fresh vegetables and new potatoes.

Iced Coffee Soufflé

Serves 4

¾ pint (425ml.) double cream
2 eggs
2 egg yolks
3 oz. (75g.) caster sugar
2 teaspoons instant coffee
2 tablespoons Tia Maria
icing sugar and powdered coffee

1 This sweet is best done in individual soufflé dishes. Prepare these by lining with double thickness greaseproof paper, so that the paper comes 1″ (2cm.) above the rim of the dish. This is so that when you remove the paper the frozen mixture will be in the shape of a soufflé.

2 Dissolve the instant coffee in a tablespoon of boiling water. Allow to cool and then add ½ pint (275ml.) of the double cream and half of the Tia Maria. Lightly whip, it must not be stiff.

3 Whisk the eggs, egg yolks and sugar until very light and fluffy. Very carefully fold this mixture into the lightly whipped cream. Pour into the prepared moulds and deep freeze for 6 - 8 hours.

4 To serve, whip up the remaining cream for piping. Remove the paper from the soufflés by dipping the dish in warm water. Using a grapefruit knife, hollow out the middle and put to one side. Pour the remaining Tia Maria into the hollow and pipe with the whipped cream. Replace the hollowed out piece and dust with a mixture of icing sugar and powdered coffee. Serve at once.

Provençal

Salisbury
Chef/proprietor *Edward Moss*

Avocat farci de Poulet fumé, gratiné

Serves 4

2 whole avocados, halved, peeled and
    finely sliced
½ small onion
8 oz. (225g.) smoked chicken, diced
    with the skin on
pinch garlic, crushed
glass white wine
2½ fl. oz. (60ml.) double cream
2½ fl. oz. (60ml.) seasoned béchamel
    sauce
4 oz. (125g.) Cheddar, grated
seasoning
chopped herbs (optional)

Variations of this dish can be made with prawns or ordinary poached chicken in place of smoked, but we find the delicious 'wood smoke' flavour that permeates the dish is lacking.

1 Take four small, flat ovenproof dishes and place chicken in each. Sprinkle lightly with a little bit of white wine, seasoning, garlic, herbs, and onion.

2 Set on a low flame on top of the oven and simmer. When warmed through and the onion has begun to soften, take the halves of avocado and place over each of the chicken mixtures. Press lightly from one end to fan the avocado a little. Pour over the cream and béchamel and sprinkle with the cheese. Place under a very hot grill and cook to a golden brown.

Duck Supremes with a Sweet and Sour Peach Sauce

Serves 4

4 large fresh duck supremes
6 fresh peaches, stoned
¼ pint (150ml.) duck stock or similar
1 tablespoon green peppercorns
sugar, to flavour
lemon juice, to flavour
wine vinegar, to flavour subtly
garlic, finely chopped
seasoning
cornflour

1 Trim all excess fat from the edge of the duck breasts. Cut round the wing bone about 1″ (2.5cm.) below the knuckle and pull back flesh to reveal 1″ (2.5cm.) of clean bone. Chop off knuckle and the adhering flesh. Score the fat on the breasts with a very sharp knife in a neat criss-cross, taking care not to cut into the flesh itself. Season and rub in a little garlic. Set under a hot grill. When the top is brown and the fat nicely crisp, turn over and finish cooking. Cook until pinky rare.

2 Make the sauce by liquidising 4 peaches (with their skin on), stock, sugar, wine vinegar and lemon juice. Set to boil gently in an enamel or stainless steel pan.

3 When the peach purée is soft, pass through a very fine strainer. Press with wooden spoon to extract all the juices. If necessary thicken to a masking consistency with a little cornflour, dissolved in white wine. Sprinkle in the green peppercorns.

4 Cut the cooked breasts into fine slices lengthways and arrange in a fan on a hot dish. Cut the remaining two peaches into fine slices and arrange on the same dish. Mask the dish lightly with the sauce. Decorate with a small sprig of tarragon or a borage flower and serve immediately.

Purée d'Angers au Porto

Serves 4

1 lb. (450g.) prunes, soaked overnight
lemon zest and juice
sugar
1 wine glass tawny port, to flavour
liquid double cream

We have converted more people to prunes with this dish than one would believe possible. The combination of flavours is quite astonishing.

1 Boil the prunes until very soft with a little lemon zest and sugar and leave to cool.

2 Destone the prunes and liquidise with the port and a little lemon juice until the mixture reaches a just pourable consistency. Pass through a fine mouli.

3 Serve in a tall glass, topped with double cream, like an Irish coffee.

The Rafters

Stow on the Wold
Chef/proprietor *Keith Maby*

Casserolettes de Fruits de Mer

Serves 4

For the pastry:
½ lb. (225g.) flour
¼ lb. (125g.) butter
salt
egg yolk
2½ fl. oz. (60ml.) water

any combination of the following,
allowing 4 oz. (125g.) per person:

lobster and/or Dublin bay prawns,
    boiled and shelled
shelled prawns or shrimps
mussels, cooked and shelled

scallops, shelled, washed, sliced and
    sautéed in butter
sole or other firm fish, filleted and
    poached in fish fumet and white wine
½ pint (275ml.) fish fumet
½ pint (275ml.) cream
2 oz. (50g.) butter
cayenne pepper, lemon juice and
    chopped parsley

Hollandaise sauce

1 Make the pastry and cover and put in the refrigerator for 1 hour. Roll out evenly to 1/5″. Cut out 4 rounds of 5″ diameter and mould each one round the outside of a well greased ramekin. Place upside down on baking tray, brush with beaten egg, prick the tops and bake for about 25 minutes at 200°C/400°F/gas 6 until golden brown. Leave to cool a little before unmolding — these are best made in advance and put to warm gently above the stove.

2 Reduce the fish fumet by two thirds and add the cream. Reduce further and whisk in the butter (which has been beaten with cooked lobster and scallop shells, or with peeled prawns and cayenne pepper and lemon juice). Warm through your fish in the sauce but do not boil. Divide into pastry cases and top with Hollandaise. Glaze quickly under a hot grill, sprinkle with parsley and serve immediately.

Breast of Pigeon with Pears and Spinach Mousse and a Port Sauce

Serves 4

4 plump pigeons
2 pears (Comice, Williams or similar),
    poached in a light syrup
1 cup port
3 oz. (75g.) butter, diced
1 lb. (450g.) fresh spinach

2 oz. (50g.) flour, sifted
1 small egg
½ pint (275ml.) milk
white wine
nutmeg, grated

1 Remove the legs from the pigeon and make a stock by browning in a hot oven with some onion, carrot and celery. Put the pan over a high heat, pour in a little white wine vinegar and reduce, scraping all the sediment off the bottom of the pan. Add 2 pints (generous litre) water, a bay leaf and a sprig of thyme. Strain and reserve, skimming when cold.

2 For the spinach mousse, destalk, wash, cook and strain well. Then throw in a little sizzling butter to dry it out. Season with salt, pepper and nutmeg. Purée in food processor, add flour and egg and keep processing while adding the milk. Pour into 4 well buttered moulds, cover and place in a Bain Marie for about 45 minutes. Keep warm.

3 Butter the pigeon inside and out and season. Roast in a hot oven for no more than 15 minutes. Keep warm but do not cook any more while making the sauce as the flesh should remain pink.

4 For the sauce, tip off any fat and deglaze with a little white wine. Add a cupful of the pear liquor and then the stock. Reduce by at least half and add the port. Reduce further and finally thicken with the butter, adding it piece by piece, shaking the pan as you do so. Check seasoning. Lastly throw in the sliced pears to warm through. To serve, turn the spinach mousses out onto 4 hot plates and arrange the sliced pigeon breasts and the pears fanning out from the mousse. Pour over sauce and serve immediately.

Ginger Moussecake with Caramel Sauce

Serves 8

For the sponge:
3 eggs
3 oz. (75g.) sugar
3 oz. (75g.) plain flour, sifted
1½ oz. (40g.) clarified butter
Rum or Kirsch

For the mousse:
3 eggs
4 oz. (125g.) sugar
4 pieces stem ginger, finely chopped
2 tablespoons of the syrup from the
  stem ginger
½ oz. (15g.) gelatine (6 leaves)
½ pint (275ml.) whipped cream

1 Light the oven at 190°C/375°F/gas 5. Butter and flour an 8″ (20cm.) tin. Whisk egg yolks and sugar until thick and fold in flour quickly but carefully, keeping the mixture as light as possible. Add the clarified butter. Pour into the tin and bake for about 25 - 30 minutes until the sponge just resists mild pressure from your finger. Turn onto cooling rack. This may be made a day in advance and kept in a tin. Before using, the sponge should be liberally soaked in rum or kirsch, and sliced horizontally.

2 Using the same tin, cover the base with sugar and sprinkle with lemon juice and 1 tablespoon water and heat until caramelised. Meanwhile, whisk the eggs and sugar until thick and add the gelatine, which has been soaked and then dissolved in a little warm water. Stir over ice until the mixture just begins to set. Add the cream, ginger and syrup and half of the mixture into

the prepared tin. Carefully place ½ of the soaked sponge on top and pour over the rest of the mousse. Finally top with the rest of the sponge. Allow to set in the refrigerator for several hours before turning out.

3 Serve with a sauce, made by melting ½ lb. (225g.) sugar with ¼ pint (125ml.) water. When completely dissolved, bring to the boil and boil until golden brown — do not burn — immediately withdraw from the stove and throw in ¼ pint (125ml.) water (mind out for the splashes) and stir until liquid. Allow to cool and you should have a pourable sauce.

Rose Tree

Bourton on the Water
Chef/proprietor *Jane Mann*

Fresh Mussels in Garlic and Cheese

Serves 8

8 - 10 mussels per person
2 tablespoons white wine
1 small onion, chopped
1 oz. (25g.) butter
½ lb. (225g.) Cheddar, grated
½ lb. (225g.) Gruyère, grated

For the garlic butter:
½ lb. (225g.) butter, softened
10 cloves garlic, crushed
ground black pepper

1 Make the garlic butter by creaming the butter with garlic and black pepper.

2 Clean and beard the mussels, being careful to throw away any dead ones.

3 Fry the onion in 1 oz. (25g.) butter. Add the white wine and when simmering add mussels. Shake while simmering until mussels are open and cooked. Allow to cool.

4 Take half of each mussel shell off and fill remaining half with the mussel and garlic butter. Arrange about 10 mussels on individual dishes. Cover with the mixed grated cheese and heat under grill until brown and bubbling.

Beef Olives Stuffed with Chicken in Horseradish Sauce

Serves 6

6 x 6 oz. (175g.) slices best braising
    beef, sliced very thinly
oil for frying
1 large onion, chopped
1 teaspoon ground ginger
1 teaspoon curry powder

1 pint (575ml.) red wine
2 tablespoons horseradish sauce
4 tablespoons cream
1 tablespoon cornflour

For the stuffing:
1½ - 2 lb. (675g. - 900g.) raw chicken,
    minced
¼ lb. (125g.) green olives, minced
salt and freshly ground pepper

1 Mix the chicken and olives together and season. Stuff the seasoned beef with the chicken mixture and tie up. Brown in oil and arrange in casserole.

2 Fry the onion, ginger and curry powder. Add wine and reduce by half. Pour over the beef olives. Seal casserole with tin foil and pop on lid. Cook very slowly at 150- 170°C/ 300 - 325°F/gas 2 - 3 for 3 hours or until tender. Remove to serving dish.

3 Mix the cornflour, cream and horseradish. Bring to the boil with the juice from the casserole and simmer till thickened.

4 Remove string from beef olives and pour sauce over. Serve with plain rice or creamed potatoes.

Honey and Walnut Roulade

Serves 6

4 eggs
¼ lb. (125g.) caster sugar
2 oz. (50g.) plain flour
3 oz. (75g.) walnuts
3 tablespoons runny honey
½ pint (275ml.) cream, whipped
icing sugar

1 Grease Swiss roll tin and heat your oven to 230°C/450°F/gas 8.

2 Beat the eggs and sugar until they stand in peaks.

3 Chop nuts and mix with the sifted flour. Fold nuts, flour and honey into beaten eggs. Put mixture into greased tin and bake until risen and just firm. Do not overcook.

4 Turn out on to a towel covered rack. When completely cool, fill with whipped cream. Carefully roll up and decorate with piped cream and brush with icing sugar.

Tailor's Eating House

Cheltenham
Chef *Chris Wickens*

Apple Soup

Serves 4

2½ pints (1¼ litres) good, strong
   chicken stock, must be fresh
1½ lb. (675g.) cooking apples, peeled
   and cored
½ teaspoonful ginger
salt and pepper

1 Clear the fat from your stock, if there is
any. Strain well into a pan and bring to the
boil.

2 Stew the apples gently in the stock until
just cooked.

3 Add salt, pepper and ginger and liquidise
the whole lot. Bring to the boil and simmer.
The soup will probably need skimming
again. Serve hot.

Jugged Pigeons

Serves 4

4 pigeons and their livers (use chicken
   livers if unavailable)
2 eggs, hard boiled and chopped
pepper, salt and pinch nutmeg
breadcrumbs
fresh thyme and parsley
grated peel 1 lemon
1 onion, chopped
¾ pint (425ml.) beer
1 oz. (25g.) butter
1 oz. (25g.) flour

1 Chop the livers and quickly fry them. Add
the eggs, nutmeg, seasonings, herbs and
lemon peel. Add enough breadcrumbs to
hold it all together.

2 Stuff the birds with the mixture and place in a casserole with the onion and beer. If the liquid doesn't completely cover the birds you can add some chicken stock. Pop into oven at 200°C/400°F/gas 6 for anything between 1 - 2 hours, depending on how tender the birds are.

3 When cooked, put the butter in a saucepan, add the flour and cook slightly to make a nice brown roux. Slowly add the juices from the casserole until the sauce is of a single cream consistency. Pour back over the pigeons and serve. *An excellent winter recipe.*

Whim Wham

Serves 1

small trifle sponge broken into tiny
   pieces
1 large tot brandy
1 large tot Cointreau
freshly squeezed orange juice
whipped cream
1 oz. (25g.) caster sugar
1 oz. (25g.) almonds

This is one of those recipes that can be made up to the chef's liking — as much or as little spirit as desired!

1 Put the almonds and caster sugar over the heat in a thick bottomed pan, stirring continuously and lightly caramelise. Remove from the heat, making sure that you have not heavily caramelised them.

2 Put the sponge into a glass bowl and add the spirit and enough orange juice to make it nice and moist. It can now be left till the last minute before serving.

3 Add the whipped cream, as much as you like, and sprinkle the caramelised almonds over the top. Serve.

Thornbury Castle

Thornbury
Chef/proprietor *Kenneth Bell*

Caveached Salmon

Serves 6

1½ lb.(875g.) centre cut of salmon

For the marinade:
6 fl. oz. (175ml.) dry white wine
1 tablespoon salt
¼ teaspoon ground pepper
juice 1 lemon
juice 1 orange
¼ onion, finely chopped
1 clove garlic, finely chopped
2 fl. oz. (50ml.) very best oil

1 Cut the salmon horizontally in half and trim completely of skin and bone, leaving two fillets weighing probably ½ lb. (225g.) each. Cut each into three little steaks, each portion should weigh between 2 - 3 oz. (50 - 75g.).

2 Mix together all the ingredients for the marinade and pour over the salmon pieces.

Put into the refrigerator. Shake the container occasionally to ensure the marinade is in contact with all sides of the salmon fillets.

3 The salmon can be eaten after 6 hours in the marinade but is at its best at 24 to 48 hours. Serve as a first course, decorated with a little salad.

Épaule d'Agneau en Melon

4 - 5 lb. (1¾ - 2¼ kilos) shoulder lamb
cooking oil
1 onion
1 carrot
rosemary
¼ pint (150ml.) consommé or brown
  stock
red wine

For the stuffing:
1 onion, finely chopped
1 oz. (25g.) butter
4 oz. (125g.) rice
¾ pint (425ml.) chicken stock
2 oz. (50g.) dried raisins
2 oz. (50g.) pine or pistachio nuts,
  shelled
garlic, chopped
salt and pepper
parsley, chopped

1 To make the stuffing, soften the onion in butter, add the rice and allow to absorb the butter. Pour over the boiling chicken stock, season, add the raisins and boil for 1 minute and cook for 17 minutes in a medium oven. At the end of this time the rice should have absorbed all the stock. Allow to cool and mix in the chopped garlic, parsley and nuts.

2 Take the shoulder of lamb and remove surplus skin and fat. Take out the bone and spread the shoulder out. Fill with the stuffing. Then make a parcel of the lamb and stuffing roughly melon shaped, securely tied with string.

3 2 hours before the meal, preheat the oven to very hot. Put a couple of tablespoons of oil into a roasting tin and place the lamb bones, carrot, onion, rosemary and lamb in the tin. Season with salt and pepper and put to roast. After 15 minutes lower heat to 200°C/400°F/gas 6 and continue roasting for 1¼ hours, basting often. Add the stock or consommé to the pan and continue cooking until done to your liking. Transfer lamb to a serving dish and remove string. Keep hot.

4 Make the gravy by adding some red wine to the roasting dish and cook for a few minutes. Strain the gravy into a small saucepan. Skim off the fat and adjust seasoning. Carve the lamb into wedges, like a melon and serve with Dauphinois potatoes and ratatouille.

Gâteau Paris-Brest

For the choux pastry:
3½ oz.(100g.) plain flour
⅓ pint (200ml.) water
2½oz. (60g.) butter
½ level teaspoon salt
3 or 4 eggs
sliced almonds

For the praline:
3 oz. (75g.) whole unblanched almonds
3 oz. (75g.) sugar

For the Chantilly cream:
1 pint (575ml.) double cream
1 oz. (25g.) sugar
Kirsh

1 Make the choux pastry by bringing the water and butter and salt to the boil. Add all the flour in one go and beat with a wooden spoon until amalgamated. Remove from heat and add eggs one by one — three may be enough but add a fourth if mixture will not fall off the spoon when filled and upturned.

2 Set oven at 200°C/400°F/gas 6. Pipe pastry onto silicon paper in a ring of about 8″ (20cm.) diameter using a ¾″ (1.5cm.) plain nozzle. Pipe another ring inside and touching first and then a third ring on top of the other two. Brush with beaten egg and sprinkle with sliced almonds. Bake for 35 minutes until thoroughly cooked. Put onto a wire rack and split open horizontally so that steam escapes.

3 To make the praline, put almonds and sugar in a heavy pan and heat until sugar caramelises. Pour onto a marble slab and leave until cool. Grind to a powder in a coffee mill or under a heavy rolling pin.

4 Beat the cream, adding sugar and Kirsch and powdered praline.

5 Assemble the gâteau by piping generous amounts of the cream over the base ring. Cover this with the top ring and pipe more cream rosettes over the top. For a richer gâteau, use butter cream or crème St. Honoré in place of the Chantilly cream.

White House

Williton
Chefs/proprietors *Dick and Kay Smith*

Chilled Aubergine Purée

Serves 4

2 - 3 aubergines (according to size)
1 clove garlic, crushed
1 tablespoon olive oil (the best you can
   find — I use Tuscan, first pressing)
1 tablespoon lemon juice
sea salt and freshly ground black
   pepper

Some years ago we happened to be in Istanbul for a few days. On the first day we spied an interesting hors d'oeuvre in the 'coffee shop' of the Sheraton Hotel; shredded and mashed aubergines with an intriguing smokey taste. We returned every subsequent day specifically to eat this dish — be warned, it can become addictive! It is a very useful recipe for aubergine lovers as it isn't cooked in masses of oil.

1 Cover the grill rack with foil and grill aubergines under full heat, turning every few minutes. When you think they are sufficiently cooked, test them by seeing if the skin has blackened and has begun to come away from the pulp, which should be soft and juicy — about 30 minutes.

2 Allow to cool a little and peel, discarding the blackened skin. Cut the flesh into 3″ (8cm.) pieces and shred using two forks — it should not be too smooth. Mix in the remaining ingredients to taste. Chill for at least 2 hours before serving. This will keep extremely well in the refrigerator and may be made on a previous day.

Fricassée de Poulet au Vinaigre

Serves 4

4 chicken supremes, cut into ½″ x 3″
   (1.5 x 8cm.) strips
2 tablespoons finely chopped shallots
4 tomatoes, roughly chopped and cored

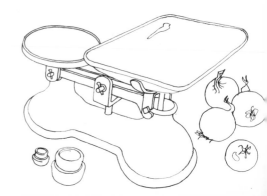

3 tablespoons raspberry vinegar
(substitute good quality wine vinegar
if unavailable)
4 tablespoons cultured cream
sea salt and freshly ground black
pepper
butter to cook
pinch cayenne and a little sugar

1 Soften the shallots in the butter. Add the tomatoes and cook gently until reduced. Put aside in separate pan.

2 Sauté the chicken breasts in butter, taking care not to overcook. Remove from pan and keep warm.

3 Deglaze the pan with the vinegar, add the shallot and tomato mixture together with the cream and, using a wooden spoon, scrape away any brown bits and incorporate into the sauce. Add the cayenne and the sugar and adjust the seasoning — the sauce should be quite piquant.

4 Return the chicken to the pan and coat with the sauce. Serve on a mound of green tagliatelli, cooked 'al dente'.

Loganberry Crème Brûlée

Serves 4

2 oz. (50g.) caster sugar
5 egg yolks
¾ pint (425ml.) thick double cream
2 oz. (50g.) natural unrefined sugar (I
find Billington Mauritius sugar from
Sainsbury's ideal)
few ounces loganberries, frozen will do
if not in season

Part of the success of this sweet is in the quality of the cream, which needs to be the heaviest you can find. We are fortunate in being able to buy what must be the 'thickest cream in the world' from a local dairy farm.

1 In a saucepan, scald the cream.

2 Beat the sugar and egg yolks with a wire whisk until thick. Pour on scalded cream and mix.

3 Return to the saucepan on a low heat, stirring constantly until thick — do not boil!

4 In 4 cocotte dishes distribute the loganberries (still frozen, if using these) and pour on the crème. Refrigerate for at least 2 hours or overnight.

5 Spread a layer of the unrefined sugar on top of each and melt till caramelised under a hot preheated grill. Return to refrigerator until serving.

Woods

Bath
Chef *Sharon Maryon-Robinson*

Mushroom Gougère with Tarragon Hollandaise   *Serves 6*

For the gougère:
1½ oz. (40g.) butter
¼ pint (150ml.) water
2 eggs
2 oz. (50g.) flour
½ oz. (15g.) cheese, finely grated
1½ oz. (40g.) cheese, cubed
salt and pepper
pinch nutmeg
pinch parsley, chopped

For the mushroom mixture:
1 onion, finely chopped
1 fat clove garlic, finely chopped
1 oz. (25g.) butter

1 lb. (450g.) baby button mushrooms
pinch nutmeg
grated rind and juice 1 lemon
splash red wine
splash sherry

For the Hollandaise:
small handful fresh tarragon leaves (or
    dried soaked in white wine and oil)
4 egg yolks
2 teaspoons warm water
½ lb. (225g.) unsalted butter, melted
squeeze lemon juice
salt and pepper

1 For the gougère, melt the butter in the water, stir in flour and seasoning. Remove to an electric mixer and beat well. Add the eggs and continue to beat for a few seconds. Stir in the cubed cheese and chopped parsley. Place on a greased baking tray in a large circle, sprinkle with grated cheese and bake in a hot oven for 10 - 15 minutes until puffed up and golden brown. Keep warm.

2 Fry the onion, garlic and mushrooms in butter. Add the remaining ingredients and boil rapidly until the mixture is thick. (Add more liquid if it gets too dry). Keep warm.

3 For the Hollandaise, whizz up egg yolks, tarragon and water in a liquidiser. Slowly pour in the melted butter, still beating. Season with salt, pepper and lemon juice. Serve a slice of warm gougère with a spoonful of the hot mushroom mixture and a blob of Hollandaise. Garnish with a sprig of watercress.

Grey Mullet Grilled with Fresh Fennel and Flamed in Pernod

Serves 4

4 medium sized grey mullet, gutted and
   descaled
1 head fennel, thinly sliced
3 lemons (or limes)
salt and pepper
oil
2 tots Pernod
watercress and chopped parsley to
   garnish
fennel branches or tops

1 Make two diagonal slits on one side of the fish and stuff the body cavity and slits with the sliced fennel.

2 Slice one lemon finely. Place the lemon slices along the body of the fish. Place the fennel branches in a baking tray and put the fish on top. Season with salt, pepper and the juice of the remaining lemons and the oil. Grill for approximately 10 minutes, until the flesh flakes from the bones — lower heat if the skin starts to burn.

3 Pour over the Pernod and flame.

4 Pop fish onto a serving dish and serve with the juices from the pan and some parsley, watercress and lemon slices to garnish. This dish is equally delicious with trout or small sea bass.

Iced Lime, Kiwi Fruit and Strawberry Terrine

Serves 8 - 10

1½ pints (875ml.) whipping cream
small tin condensed milk
juice 6 limes and grated rind 3 limes
3 kiwi fruit, cut in half
¼ lb. (125g.) strawberries, halved if
   large
10 oz. (275g.) digestive biscuits,
   crushed
5 oz. (150g.) butter, melted

1 Mix the digestives with the butter and press into a 12″ (30cm.) terrine tin (with collapsing sides), making sure all sides are well covered. Reserve some biscuits for the top. Bake for 5 - 10 minutes till crisp and brown. Leave to cool.

2 Whip the cream lightly and add the condensed milk, rind and lime juice and mix till thick.

3 Layer the lime mixture with the kiwi fruit and strawberries in the tin, so that when a slice is cut you get a transverse section of the fruits in each portion. Cover with the reserved biscuit mixture and freeze until firm.

4 Turn out and slice. Serve plain or with a fresh fruit sauce.

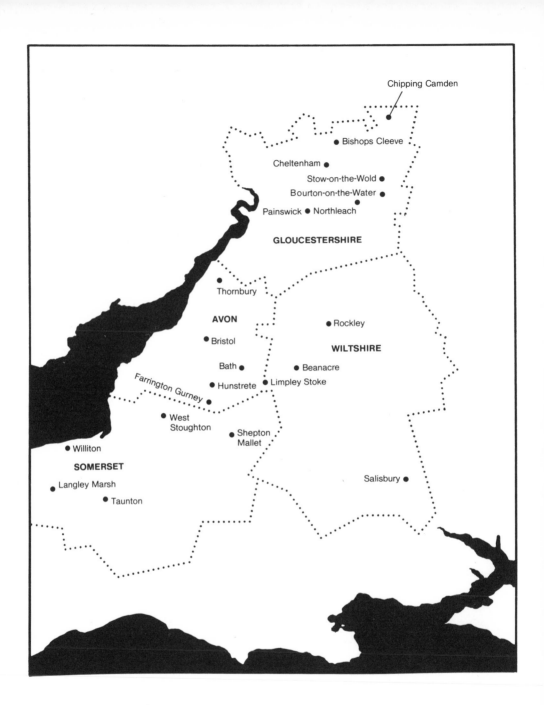

Chipping Camden

Bishops Cleeve

Cheltenham ●

Stow-on-the-Wold ●
Bourton-on-the-Water ●

Painswick ● Northleach

GLOUCESTERSHIRE

Thornbury

AVON

● Bristol

Rockley

WILTSHIRE

Bath ● ● Beanacre

Farrington Gurney ● Hunstrete ● Limpley Stoke

● West
Stoughton

Shepton
Mallet

● Williton

SOMERSET

Salisbury ●

● Langley Marsh

● Taunton

Restaurant Addresses

Ainslie's	— 12 Pierrepont St., Bath, Avon.	(0225) 61745
Anthony's	— 87 Whiteladies Road, Bristol, Avon.	(0272) 738930
Beaujolais	— 5 Chapel Row, Bath, Avon.	(0225) 23417
Beechfield House	— Beanacre, Wiltshire.	(0225) 703700
Bistro Twenty One	— Cotham Road South, Kingsdown, Bristol, Avon.	(0272) 421744
Blostin's	— 29 Waterloo Road, Shepton Mallet, Somerset.	(0749) 3648
Bowlish House	— Wells Road, Shepton Mallet, Somerset.	(0749) 2022
Castle	— Castle Green, Taunton, Somerset.	(0823) 72671
Cleeveway House	— Evesham Road, Bishops Cleeve, Glos.	(024 267) 2585
Country Elephant	— Painswick, Glos.	(0452) 813564
Country Friends	— Market Place, Northleach, Glos.	(045 16) 421
Crane's	— 90 - 92 Crane Street, Salisbury, Wiltshire.	(0722) 3471
Danielle	— The Bridge, Limpley Stoke, Wiltshire.	(022 122) 3150
Eethuys	— West Stoughton, Somerset.	(0934) 712527
Flowers	— 27 Monmouth Street, Bath, Avon.	(0225) 313774
Harveys	— 12 Denmark Street, Bristol, Avon.	(0272) 277665
The Hole in The Wall	— 16 George Street, Bath, Avon.	(0225) 25242
Homewood Park	— Hinton Charterhouse, Bath, Avon.	(022 122) 2643
Hunstrete House	— Hunstrete, Nr. Bristol, Avon.	(076 18) 578
Keith Floyd's	— 6 Chandos Road, Redland, Bristol, Avon.	(0272) 734901
Kings Arms	— Chipping Camden, Glos.	(0386) 840256
Langley House	— Langley Marsh, Somerset.	(0984) 23318
Loaves and Fishes	— Rockley, Wiltshire.	(0672) 53737
Michael's	— 129 Hotwell Road, Bristol, Avon.	(0272) 276190
Old Parsonage	— Farrington Gurney, Avon.	(0761) 52211
The Priory	— Weston Rd., Bath, Avon.	(0225) 858476
Provençal	— 14 Ox Row, Market Place, Salisbury, Wiltshire.	(0722) 28923
Rafters	— Park Street, Stow on the Wold, Glos.	(0451) 30200
Rose Tree	— Riverside, Bourton on the Water, Glos.	(0451) 20635
Tailor's Eating House	— 4 Cambray Place, Cheltenham, Glos.	(0242) 41186
Thornbury Castle	— Thornbury, Avon.	(0454) 412647
White House	— Long Street, Williton, Somerset.	(0984) 32306
Woods	— 9 Alfred Street, Bath, Avon.	(0225) 314812

Index

Cookery books from
Absolute Press

The Restaurant Recipe Book — £2.95

The first of the cookery books featuring recipes from West Country restaurants.

'**How the editor has persuaded such notables as these to give up the secrets which have made their establishments so exclusive is beyond my comprehension**'. *Ray Tennyson, Somerset & West Monthly.*

'**The Restaurant Recipe Book is strictly for best. It is the sort ot tome you reach for when entertaining and want to impress with a menu of gourmet dimensions.**' *Sally Rowat, Glos. and Avon Life.*

'**. . . a lasting souvenir to experiment with West Country cooking.**' *Gail Duff.*

Floyd's Food — £2.95

Keith Floyd, whose work is featured in 'The Restaurant Recipe Book', is a man of many talents. Restaurateur, writer, TV chef and radio personality. His excellent cookery book is for all those who want to enjoy their cooking.

'**Keith Floyd adds a dash of originality to his first cookbook. These are recipes from a restaurateur, stamped with a personal style which offers much food for thought.**' *Caterer and Hotelkeeper.*

'**. . . a wonderful and unusual selection of recipes, many of which are astonishingly simple**' *Andrew Langley, Bath & West Evening Chronicle.*

Vegetarian Cuisine — £5.95

To be published in November 1982.
If you have ever been at a loss to know what to cook when vegetarian friends come to dinner, then this is the book that will help you out. Recipes from the finest vegetarian chefs in the country laid out in easy style to help in the planning of a meal. A refreshing and delightful innovation in the world of vegetarian cookery books. A must for the bookshelves of all serious cooks, whether vegetarian or meat eating.

In preparation: '**The London Restaurant Recipe Book**' — recipes from the best of London restaurants.

If you would like to obtain any of the above titles they may be ordered through any bookshop or direct from Absolute Press, 14 Widcombe Crescent, Bath. BA2 6AH. Please enclose a cheque or Postal Order for the correct amount plus 30 pence postage.